All Ways Walk Cheerfully

Peter Schweiger

Cover image courtesy of Michael Goldhill.

ISBN: 9798846138438

PublishNation
www.publishnation.co.uk

This book is dedicated to my wife, definitely my better half, who has kept me well fed and restrained me from getting into too many concerns.

Author's Note

Also to those who want to All Ways Walk Cheerfully.

The first part is memoir and the rest my daily diary from 1981.

Many of these steps were written to stand alone so please accept the repetition in places.

Table of Contents

Step 1

First Steps

In the beginning of my life were two German Jewish refugees from The Nazis. My father's brother's dead body was found by a railway track near Heidelberg a week after he had been released from prison in 1935. He had been sentenced to a years imprisonment for using an air gun to shoot a uniformed Nazi official who was stopping people from coming into his fathers shoe shop. He just had a bruise on his thigh, so not a serious injury. It did not need a great detective to find out who had fired the shot. My Uncle had shot from his bedroom window. My father felt it best to leave Germany because of the anti semitism and he felt he was a marked man as his brother was in the Communist party. My father first went to Amsterdam in the Netherlands and made his way to England where he had contacts and could get a job in a shoe shop in the East End of London. He told me he had ten shillings when he arrived in England.

My mother was born in 1919 and grew up in Wiesbaden Germany. Her father was the director of an organisation that gave working people holidays subsidised by their employers. Her family lived in a large house opposite the town park. Her father was dismissed from his job in 1933 and they had to live on a small pension. Conditions for Jews steadily got more unpleasant. My mother had been to the Grammar school and had good friends that she had reunions with after the war. After school she trained as a nursery school teacher at a Jewish institution. Segregation had been imposed on further education.

My mother had a younger brother, Franz and when he was 17 he was sent to Buchenwald concentration camp for six months. In 1938 a farmer in Leicestershire offered him a job as a farm labourer. There was scheme to enable Jews to come to Britain if they had job offers where there was a shortage. Franz wrote back to his parents and sister how pleasant life was in England and that encouraged my mother to come to England where she was given a job as a nanny with a bank manager's family in Bognor Regis in 1939. They helped her find a job with the Columbia Road Nursery school in Whitechapel, London. With the outbreak of war the school was evacuated to Waddesden Manor, a magnificent stately home near Aylesbury Buckinghamshire. Talk about falling on your feet! There she was assistant head teacher with the cockney kids who had never seen the countryside and had a whole new world to discover. Milk came from huge animals called cows and not from bottles and so much more. My mother would meet up with other refugees when on her days off she could go by train to London. One family in particular from Wiesbaden lived in Hampstead and it could have been through them she heard about the Barn House.

My parents met at the Barn House in Brockweir, near Tintern on the English and Welsh boarder. Two Quaker ladies offered refugees in London, a working holiday break away from war torn London in 1943. Our family kept in touch with them and would go there on holiday until they eventually died. Quakerism attracted my parents because of the attitude to reconciliation rather than hatred which many Jews felt. Quakers had been persecuted for not agreeing to swear oaths, for instance. It is not necessary when one speaks the truth always. George Fox who started the Society of Friends of Jesus later called Quakers because when they spoke some were so wound up they quaked. George Fox had worked for a shoemaker in his youth before

2

he took up the cudgels against the Established Church. He felt no need for Clergy if everyone had something of God in them and like Martin Luther there is a direct line to God without an intermediary.

My parents married in 1944 and I was conceived in the war and born in the peace of October 1945. Times were tough, but my father was resourceful and could work from the rented home in Golders Green near London. He made foot supports to go in people's shoes. The foot supports took away the pain in customers feet. That is how All Ways Walk Cheerfully started. He used a room to see customers and could make them there. He had a receptionist and my mother was busy looking after me. My mother also tracked down several of her cousins who had also escaped Nazi Germany and we had outings visiting them in North West London. Customers/patients would phone my father at all times of the day and night to complain about their feet and their other concerns. That was stressful for my mother. She was glad when my father took a lease on a shop in Blandford Street, just off Baker Street in London. My brother Martin was born in 1949. My father would take me sometimes to the shop. We sat upstairs on the bus and I could see into the big bomb site at 55 Baker Street where army trucks were parked.

A narrow passage led to the front door of the shop. To the right was a high counter and straight ahead on the wall a huge crocodile skin. Stairs led down to the basement where some shoemakers worked, and another little back room with a doorway into a mews. I would help by straightening thin nails using a small hammer on a tiny anvil that I still have. It taught me not to knock my fingers. The nails were reused by the shoemakers when they were pulling the shoe uppers over the wooden lasts. My reward was a cup of Oxo. I still enjoy it. Mr Cooper had been trained by my father to measure feet and from those measurements make lasts. The shoes were made over those. He had a round jovial face and was still working for the firm when I took over running it in 1972. Mr Wilson was another long term worker who started with the firm in 1932. He was forever puffing on his pipe whose fumes filled the workshop. Very proud that he had taught himself how to make paper shoe patterns. As a result he would never show others, because if he had done it others could figure it out for themselves.

Shoemaker's work bench

Step 2

School Leaver

Unlike my younger brother Martin I was never near the top of the class and I did not pass my 11 plus. My parents felt I would do better in life if they sent me to a private Grammar School rather than the local Secondary Modern School. The Kings School Harrow was a lengthy bus journey from Golders Green but it was fun being upstairs at the front with my class mate Richard who would get on at Hendon Central. My best result was in the 3rd year when I had ten passes with four distinctions in The College of Preceptors exam. I was awarded with a book as a prize. At O level GCE in the 5th year I only got 4 passes. I had rested on my laurels. My parents enabled me to transfer to St. Nicholas Grammar School in Northwood where I joined the 6th form when I had sufficient O levels.

I was fed up with exams in the 6th form and had no clear idea about what I could do. The careers master heard my desire to get away from London. My parents had often taken my brother and me on holiday to places in the country and we had walked in woods and collected mushrooms to eat. I wanted a vocation, possibly in the Civil Service. I was attracted by the potential job security and the pension scheme. The Careers master suggested Customs and Excise or the Forestry Commission. The latter attracted me, so I applied. The interview was six months away so I worked with my father in his shop where shoes were made to measure. I did all sorts of jobs like listing old shoes that had been stored. Some were Victorian elegant ladies boots with hand sewn beads, others great big black orthopaedic shoes with six inch cork raises. The most tiring part of the job was commuting especially going home on crowded trains.

My father took me for lunch at interesting places, such as the basement vegetarian restaurant run by Mrs Hope. Sometimes we would meet customers or Harley Street doctors who sent customers to us. He also showed me his favourite statue in Paddington Street Gardens. It was of a small boy mending his shoe made of white marble and titled The Crossing Sweeper. We would sometimes go to the Wallace Collection or on bus trips to see Surgical Appliance Officers in Hospitals. His business partner would give me Kit Kats and encourage me to stay in the business. My itchy feet wanted to get away. I did not feel comfortable with the rest of the team of a dozen being "Daddies boy"

I did not know at the time but there were four thousand applicants for forty places for training as a Forester with the Forestry Commission. Minimum qualifications were five O levels. I had two A levels in Economics and Geography. One of My two references was Fred Willey, Minister of Agriculture in Harold Wilson's government who I knew through Golders Green Quaker Meeting. The other Joe Sewell was a Director of Price Waterhouse, accountants. I knew him through Harrow Quaker Meeting. At the interview in Savile Row I was asked questions such as what is brashing? Glad I had read about it. It is cutting away the lower branches on trees to give access and reduce the knots in timber.

For two years I worked piece work in Hampshire. It was the hardest I ever worked. Sheer monotonous slog sweating stooping, back breaking, with a big curved rip hook/sickle cutting grass, brambles and blackthorn away from small trees. That was during the summer. In the winter the gang and I would clear scrub for planting also on piece work. The arising would be burnt and the fires would burn for days. It was all done with hand tools such as four pound axes, slashers or bill hooks. The Forester would set the piece work rate and it was a slog to make more than the day rate. If you weren't sweating you weren't working. We would help each other out if we had easier or tougher areas. One evening a week we would play darts in the local pub. When it rained we had a shed with a stove and a dartboard. They say a good darts player is the sign of a wasted youth but I am rusty now. I am still in touch after 50 years with some of the gang.

By contrast the two years at Forester Training School were much easier. No piece work and we were paid £4.75 a week and accommodated near picturesque Capel Curig, North Wales. Just a dozen of us in my year from most parts of England and Northern Ireland. The syllabus had forty subjects and my favourite was tree climbing to collect seeds. The harnesses and ropes gave a sensation of safety as we bounced about in the branches.

Britain had not yet joined the Common Market and there were no jobs available in England or Wales. Many of my year went on Voluntary Service Overseas. I heard about a Forestry Officers job becoming vacant after a year in the London Borough of Hillingdon where I lived.

To have a good chance I worked for the borough as a tractor driver and chainsaw operator until the interview. At the interview I suggested the thousand acres of woodlands could be managed in the way that Windsor Forest operated. They sold as much of the produce as possible. I was not accepted because it was "too commercial" Some of the suggestions that I made then have been implemented.

My father had died some years before and his business partner had always encouraged me to return. I had seen that the grass was not always greener on the other side of the fence. I weighed up the pros and cons of returning to the family firm. There I could be my own boss eventually and control my future. Making footwear that would help people to walk better, more cheerfully, and also pay more than the agricultural rates. I did not want to develop into a huge business like Clarkes but stay small and have direct contact with my customers.

In September 1970 I returned to the firm. To get over the misery of commuting I took to reading. The first book was "The Good Soldier Schweik". It is hilarious about a simple soldier who always finds the best in any situation including when he is jailed.and said,

"The cell floor is so wonderfully flat".

The Forestry training philosophy was that one could not manage unless you could do the job yourself. I therefore learnt as much as I could about the different stages of shoemaking. Genial Frank Cooper showed me how to fit up the wooden lasts over which shoes were made. My father had taught him when he was discharged from the army. Frank had been a prisoner of war in Japan. When the Americans liberated the camp they sent in food first by parachute. Frank had been hit by the shackle of one that smashed his ankle. He needed specially made footwear and was sent by his hospital to my father to have a pair made. That was how he got introduced. He did not have a job and said he was willing to learn.

Mr Wilson the pattern cutter had been with the firm since 1932 and had taught himself. He did not want to show others the mystery of how he pressed the paper against the lasts and created a perfect fit.

Instead I went on an evening course at The Cordwainers Technical College in Mare Street, Hackney to learn pattern cutting. There I met other students who I knew in later life such as Rodney Freed of the ballet shoe makers, and Jimmy Choo who is very well known for fashion shoes. At Cordwainers I did other courses. Closing is sewing the pieces of leather together to make the uppers, factory making using machinery to pull the uppers over the lasts and attaching the soles and a course on Works management.

Once a week I would go to a retired shoemaker who lived in Purley and from scratch made a pair of brown leather shoes for myself. That was the best test.

In July 1972 my father's partner retired. In the months preceding I had thought the prospect to be overwhelmingly daunting and had become very depressed. My doctor prescribed anti depressant medicine and slowly I came to realise that what ever happened I should just "Enjoy it". What a simple philosophy. Two words. Rough or smooth. The staff thought I had pushed the partner out somehow and threatened to resign. I gave them a pay rise and all except the book keeper stayed.

I was 26 and told myself that if William Pitt the younger could be Prime Minister at that age, I could manage a small firm.

To replace the book keeper I advertised in the Evening Standard and several people applied. The brightest was appointed and he proved to be a thief. He had told me about a person who revived businesses in exchange for 10% of the turnover. Without me knowing he then started to help himself. The auditors were put off checking our books for a couple of years, but when they saw what he was doing advised me to dismiss him. I was loathe to because I had made him a director. My wife was called to a meeting just two days after she had given birth to our daughter. There she was made a director and the crooked book keeper dismissed with our auditor acting as chairman. The book keeper had the cheek to sue for unfair dismissal. I called in the Fraud squad who launched a criminal case against him. At the Court his barrister called me "An Amiable Dupe" That riled, because I had trusted him. The Judge said it was clearly theft in the same way as if a taxi driver were to take you on a roundabout route to push up the fare. He was sentenced to two years imprisonment and ordered to repay some of the money. He did for a while and then also came and asked if he could repay by working for me. I said, "No!"

The firm had customers whose families had had shoes made for them for several generations. James Taylor and Son were established in 1857 when James Taylor had come to London from Garboldisham in Suffolk. He must have been quite well heeled because he was able to afford a lease on 82 Great Portland Street in London's West End. It was then a fashionable shopping street on a par with Jermyn Street.

Many eminent and wealthy customers graced the shop including John Lewis, D.H Evans and other heads of Department stores.

My father bought James Taylor and Son with his business partner in 1952. The lease in Great Portland Street had expired and the grandsons Frank and Ernest wanted to retire. My father had a shop in Blandford Street near Baker Street and so could accommodate James Taylor & Son and trade using their name.

My father also won a contract to supply hospital patients on the NHS. Each year the contract had to be renewed and prices submitted for hundreds of shoe and repair items. A big chore. If the item was too high compared to the average submitted by other firms the price would be reduced. If accepted then maybe we could have tendered for more.

There were green leather benches in the shop and real aristocrats would sit with the NHS patients and say "Oh Me Feet" and compare their problems. There were a few red leather chairs too and I thought of the green benches for the Commons and the red for the Lords.

A Harley Street doctor asked me to attend Paul Getty in the London Clinic. He needed shoes to be made for his swollen feet. His room was on the top floor and he had lots of videos. He liked the quality of Betamax and recommended it to me. I am glad I did not follow his advice because that system did not last long. I took his measurements and a pair of lasts were made. Our Polish last maker showed them to a reporter from the Evening Standard and Mr Getty was mentioned in an article. The next time I visited him he told me off for using his name as an advertisement. Fortunately he ordered another pair of shoes. He died some years ago, but I have since been to work parties on his estate with the Chiltern Society where we planted a box tree plantation.

After that I was careful not to name drop and yet that was all reporters seem to want.

Step 3

Learning Curve

During the first six months after I had left school and worked at the shop with my father I had not been interested in what was going on around me. I did relatively unskilled jobs such as fitting support pads in shoes, or filing repair tickets.

It was in 1970 when I returned after my time working in Forestry and Hillingdon Council that I started to find out about the mysteries of shoemaking. If I was to run the firm eventually I felt I should know about the whole craft. That was the philosophy at the Training school. Before you manage you should know how to do the work.

My father's partner, Ruby Hiatt, was running the firm after he died. She had been like an auntie in my childhood and was pleased when I changed my mind and returned. She was happy to let me go on courses. Twice a week I would leave early and go on the underground and bus to the Cordwainers Technical College in Mare St. Hackney. I did pattern cutting and the first style we did was a ladies high heel court. Just the style that is so damaging to toes. The instructor was an older woman called Miss Facey and she had known my father when he was on courses there in 1939.

Friday afternoons I did a course on machine shoemaking and made a pair of black lace up shoes for myself. I was conscious of the mistakes in them but no one else was.

Another course was Works Management and it covered a lot of what I had learnt at Forestry School.

George Bell was a shoemaker who had had a business in Connaught Street near Marble Arch. He passed his customers on to us when he retired. On a Tuesday I would go by train to Purley and use the phone box when I reached the station. I would hang up after two rings and his wife would come with the car and take me to their home. George and I would be in the conservatory where he guided me in every stage of shoemaking. We measured my feet, made lasts and patterns. I brought some mid brown calf leather and lining material and cut out the leather so that it would not stretch lengthways. I used his Singer sewing machine to "close" the uppers. Closing is turning something that was flat into 3D. Pulling the uppers over the lasts with "Lasting pinchers" and hammering in thin nails to hold the leather was a skill. Holding the nails between the lips and spitting them into the other hand was a game I learnt.

The shoes were welted so the uppers were sewn with an awl first making a hole through the strip of leather called a welt and into a ridge in the insole. The work was done sitting on a low stool with a leather strap going under my foot and holding the last firmly against my thigh. The insole was hidden so it took judgement to get exactly the correct depth. The welt ran around the front of the shoe from one side of the heel to the other. The welt was marked every eighth of an inch evenly with a gimping wheel with sharp points. The hollow between the welts was filled with waxed felt. The leather sole was sewn on using strands of hemp six foot or more long that were twisted and bound with beeswax to make a thread. Each end had a thin bristle. The bristle could be from a hog, but I had clear plastic ones. It took about an hour to go round each shoe poking the bristles into the holes made by the awl and pulling the hemp through. Each time crossing over so that the threads locked and the sole could not come off if one stitch broke. Looking down on the welt the stitches made a nice row of dots.

The next part was to build the heels with layers of thick leather. The layers were glued with neoprene and then nailed. To reduce the weight a hole was cut in the middle of the layers, or "Lifts" as they are called. The heels were trimmed with a very sharp blade and made to match in shape and height. The final layer was a rubber one because it was less slippery and longer wearing than leather. The edges of the soles and heels were stained brown to match the uppers and rubbed with hot metal iron tools.

Getting the lasts out of the shoes is hard work. A block at the top has to be unscrewed and pulled away and a special hook inserted into a hole in the back of the last. It took a lot of pressure on the finger tips pulling the sides of the shoe up away from the hook that extended under a foot. When nails had been forgotten to be removed when lasting or the nails in the heels were too long and went into the lasts, it was a terrible struggle.

When the shoes were off the lasts, the insoles felt like Braille where nail holes had been. The insoles had to be sanded down with emery cloth on a curved stick. Another thin layer of leather the shape of the insole was stuck in with rubber solution. It smelt and the fumes could give one a "high". The shoes were then polished and laces put in before I put them on. They were on and off my feet for the next twenty years.

When I took on trainees I let them make a pair of shoes for themselves first, before letting them work on customers shoes. The more shoes a maker made the better they got. They also got faster and were eventually on piecework.

They could work at home. They were given the lasts, uppers and the leather for insoles, soles and heel lifting to work with. The order form would give all the measurements and instructions. Some makers came to the shop once a week to deliver and collect more work. Some moved away from London and we could post work to them. One was in Devon, another in Sussex. I did visit them and we enjoyed the reunion.

Step 4

Daunting Months

The firm had been struggling financially ever since my father fell ill and then died in 1968. Ruby was very kind hearted and did not want to put up prices. So many customers she felt would not be able to afford shoes. I had rejoined the firm in September 1970 and was learning the craft. At the same time I could see why there were problems. Inflation had started to grip the economy. Prices for materials and wages for staff were going up and the firm was trading on an overdraft guaranteed by the freehold of the building. Ruby thought it best to retire at the start of 1972 and to sell her share in the building to my mother. Luckily my mother had inherited money from a cousin in South Africa called Ceasar Schlessinger. He had been a director of Lever Brothers. A price for the building was agreed and because of the poor state of the business Ruby was paid nothing for that. After all despite the value of the stock the overdraft was higher.

I had doubts that I could cope with the multiple tasks of managing the business when Aunty Ruby was due to retire in July 1972. All the staff were older than me and I got the feeling they thought I had pushed Ruby out. The book keeper also resigned and the rest of the staff threatened to. I had a severe dose of depression and my doctor put me on medication. Eventually it dawned on me that life was simple. A philosophy of two words. Enjoy it. The ups and the downs. Then help others to enjoy theirs.

Step 5

The Shop

A living museum was how I regarded the shop. Since it was built in 1790 it had been a shop with the owners living above. Close to the crossroads of Marylebone High Street with Paddington Street it faced a fishmonger whose displays of fish were changed daily. They even had a live mermaid on the marble slabs once. Well she was a model for some advert and a photographer was busy.

The pavement outside the shop is raised with a white marble edge surrounding the red square tiles and a glazed trap door.

A big single pane of glass had been installed by my father to replace three pieces and in 1954 was the largest plate glass in any shop. The shoe display was changed monthly and had seasonal themes.

A well worn oak lintel to the left of the window marked the entrance and an iron gate with bars that had been repainted many times making them much thicker than originally and opened against the wall. It was closed at night and the brass knob on the latch slid sideways rather than twisted. That fooled many an opportunist trying to get into the porch.

The glazed shop door had a big handle that had been re polished so often that the chrome had worn off exposing shiny brass. The Inside handle was more ornate. I would polish the handle often and wish for a certain number of new bespoke orders. A bit like Aladin and his lamp. Sometimes my wish would come true.

A wrought iron circular light fitting hung from the high ceiling on chains and had four white globes. City of London coats of arms decorated the rim. I had seen it on a cart of a scrap metal merchant as he led his horse along the street calling out "Old iron, old iron". Paid two pounds for it in 1972 and had it installed in the shop to replace strip lighting.

The shop counter was made of plywood and then had a larger board put on top to make room for the autograph till. A wooden box with a draw for cash that pinged when opened and a window on top with a paper roll below that cleverly scrolled on each time the drawer was opened. We had to write details of the transaction on the paper and at the end of the day count the cash and see if it matched the totals written on the roll. So often we had forgotten to write down transactions when considering how much change to give instead. Taking cash was when I thought of myself as a shopkeeper. The wooden box did baffle would be thieves who did not recognise it as a till.

Along one wall were three leather benches with illuminated display cabinets separating them. They were covered with green Connelly hide and in front of the shop window chairs with red leather seats. I thought of the chairs for Lords and the green benches for the Commoners. So often we did have men and women from all classes who commiserated about their painful feet. In front of each bench was a wooden footstool with a green seat to match. The angled foot plate made it easier for laces to be tied.

The Counter with Till

Step 6

Jury Service

With the help of jolly Mr Cooper I was learning how to fit up lasts. The drawings of customers feet were given to me and I had to find an old pair of lasts of similar size and then adjust them. It was 1971 and I had a letter instructing me to go for Jury Service at a local Crown Court. What an experience. The building was impressive and the crowds of people called for service were effectively organised by a clerk into waiting rooms. What a lot of time we seemed to spend there. My Jury Service was for a few days a week spread over a month. Sometimes I was called to a case and then asked to leave again because of some objection by the defendant. I did get on the jury of two cases. The first was of a woman whose car had gone over the central reservation of the M1 on a frosty morning. The barrister for the prosecution made such a convincing case that she was guilty, and the the barrister for the defence was also very convincing that she was not guilty of dangerous driving. The judges summing up left us baffled. Well we found her not guilty of dangerous driving because the road was icy and only a professional driver could have coped with the situation in which she had found herself.

The other case was of a man who was accused of stealing petrol by driving away from a filling station without paying. It happened I knew the place and it gave Green Shield stamps. If he had paid he would have got some and a receipt. We found him guilty. It was pointed out that he would have a criminal record and damage his career as a chemist. It taught me to always ask for a receipt when I bought anything for cash.

I also thought what an awful waste of time Jury Service had been. I did not want to do it again, so I delayed paying rates on my home until I had a summons. That way it showed that I was a person of bad character, and so not likely to be called again, and it worked.

Step 7

1 and 1 equals 11 / Mr 10%

Mr Whitehead the book keeper resigned when Ruby retired. I advertised in the Evening Standard and had a stream of applicants. Only one was positive and sounded inspirational so I employed him. Mr Malik was very energetic and worked in the front of the shop, so saw everything and yet had columns of figures to add up. He used an adding machine, something new to the firm and he had rolls of paper that he cross checked. Being older than me I was easily persuaded by him. He would speak from experience and suggest what in my mind were dubious ideas. That is where the one plus one equals eleven comes from. Large companies would do all sorts of things that would be hidden by their accountants. Delay the audit by a year was one suggestion to save the expense sounded attractive. However it was only to hide the amount he was stealing from the firm. He had suggested that he would be able to make the firm prosper and in exchange have 10% of the turnover. I had never agreed and he did not have anything in writing to say so. Nevertheless he took cash whenever customers paid that way. I suspected what was happening but thought it was better the devil you know than the one you don't.

When our auditors did eventually come and examine the books they told me what he was doing. Being a small firm there had to be at least two directors and he was the other one. We called a meeting with him, the auditor, and my wife who had given birth to our daughter just two days before. It had not been easy to come into the shop on the train and climbing up to the third floor office. At the meeting he was asked to explain why he was taking so much money from the firm. He tried saying he was on 10% Commission as well as his salary. The auditor said he had never had that agreed and he was stealing. I then dismissed him as the book keeper and director. My wife was appointed director. I had to find a new book keeper and advertised in the Quaker magazine The Friend. I hoped that I would find a more trustworthy person and I did.

Meanwhile Mr Malik put in a claim for unfair dismissal. That had me worried for a time, until the auditor suggested I call in the Police. The Fraud Squad were very helpful and soon had the claim for unfair dismissal quashed. They investigated and a trial was set up in the Southwark Crown Court. I was called an Amiable Dupe by the defence barrister, which rankled. Still it was probably true. The judge in the summing up said it was similar to a taxi driver taking a long route to a destination to boost his fare. That was common theft. Mr Malik was sentenced to two years imprisonment. He had a wife and baby daughter and lived in a flat close to Harrods. The Fraud Squad had followed him going to a Casino in Berkeley Square where he had gambled away the money.

He did repay some of the money when he was released and presumably had a job. To my surprise he came and visited me in the shop. He said he was sorry for what he had done and suggested he could repay the firm faster by working again for it. I had been taken in by him before and did not want to risk it again. Anyway we had found a new book keeper in the mean time.

Step 8

Best Bookkeepers

After my problems with my crooked bookkeeper I advertised in the Quaker magazine "The Friend". That brought Kenneth Goode a retired schoolteacher who had the most amazing handwriting. As it was 1980 our accounts were still all handwritten and his lovely legible script was a delight for the auditors. Sadly Kenneth had to resign due to ill health after only six months, so I advertised again in "The Friend" and Gerald Joyce came to work with us for the next ten years. He had worked for a bank but was made redundant. He was so loyal and thorough and each month would give me the accounts so we knew how the firm was doing. His daughter Shirley also helped me by typing my letters that I would dictate on a tape. She worked for the British Council in Portland Place and I would pop over and collect and deliver the letters. The British Council at that time was run by Brian Eastman, who later became a film producer of TV series such as Poroit and other "whodunnits"

He also came to us to have boots made for his challenging feet and legs.

Gerald found it harder to work due to ill health and so retired after ten years, to be followed by another Quaker, Alan Rowland. He was a retired headmaster who had been in Rumallah School in the Lebanon where he had many scary moments.

Computers were becoming the norm in businesses in 1990 and so we felt we had to as well. Alan had some experience and my wife and I wanted to learn. The Government were giving grants, so we applied. My older half brother Frank was a qualified computer instructor so we were able to have his services, once a week. He would drive over from Billericay to our home in Amersham.

We bought an Amstrad computer with a green screen and a laser printer. When the printer was delivered it was so heavy that it fell off the back of the lorry. No it was not stolen. We did get a replacement. My brother Frank ploughed his way through the course, but at times it was only due to our snoring dog that we kept awake. We went and bought an accounting program called Ability Plus from a man who said he loved it. Well it takes all sorts. Alan Rowland was able to do in two days the work Gerald needed the whole week. Computerisation speeded up the process enormously. Alan ran the accounts for ten years and for the last few years my wife helped in the shop. She made sure the till balanced and was careful with all the shop expenses. The staff sometimes commented to me that my wife was over careful with the biscuits.

Step 9

4 Paddington Street

3 Owning families in Two hundred years.

Early days.

That River Thames was absolutely enormous as the ice melted from over the Chiltern Hills at the end of the last Ice Age. Huge cliffs of ice were crashing down depositing huge rocks that had been torn off Norwegian mountains and carried for years to England. All the streams of melt water carried rocks and stones, gravel and sand that dropped here and there as the water flowed to the sea. In the vast fullness of time deep beds of gravel and sand were left. The area to the north of what became London, beds of clay and sand were deposited. Thousands of years later humans settled in what became London. Invading tribes found they could cross the Thames there and so travellers came and those who chose to live there could trade. Food for furs or accommodation for acorns.

The Romans built a fort on a hillock close by and leaping forwards a thousand years the Normans built a massive stone castle. More and more people came to live and trade and London grew with more and more houses. They were built on the fields. The tracks that led to London had houses built along them and then the fields in-between had streets of houses. Churches often gave the areas a district a name and so it was that St Mary by the Bourne over the centuries became St. Marylebone.

The Bourne was the stream that millennium before had deposited layers of sand in the area. At the end of the seventeen hundreds builders hit on the idea of digging out the sand to make cellars. The sand was yellow and used to make bricks to build the houses. The bricks were fairly soft because they did not have a lot of clay in the mixture.

And so it was that the road from Marylebone towards Paddington was developed. It had to cross an old burial pit that had been created after the plagues. Some 80 thousand people had been buried there. The road was called Paddington Street and linked Marylebone High Street with Baker Street. The continuation towards Paddington was called Crawford Street. London in the late eighteenth century was noisy, smelly and congested. There were no drains or piped water. Heating was with open fires using hornbeam logs that were brought in from the forests. The smoke from the chimneys usually blew out towards the east.

Houses were numbered so that people could have addresses and directories complied. Kelly's 1790 listed 4 Paddington Street as having Robert Bell and his occupation was shoemaker. There were six other houses in Paddington Street with shoemakers. What a lot of competition. On the north side the house numbers started at One and ran sequentially up to Baker Street and then back down the other side. A big gap where the burial ground was. No 4 like all its neighbours had railings next to the narrow pavement to prevent people falling down into the basement area. Under the pavement three arched vaults served as storage for fuel. At the back of the building was another area open to the sky with the privy at one end. The bucket from that would be emptied in to a "honey wagon". A man with a horse and cart would collect the human waste and tip it somewhere. Probably on fields as fertiliser.

The Howard de Walden Estate owned the farms in the area and had built up the fields with fine houses in a grid pattern. The largest houses were along Portland Place which ran north to south. Parallel to it was and is Harley Street and Wimpole Street also with larger houses. The streets running east to west tended to have less grand buildings. Paddington Street is a terrace block of three storey houses with grand arches over the first floor windows, reminiscent of the side of Buckingham Palace. The ceilings in the ground floor are 12 foot high as are the first floor, the second is lower and the third floor about 8 foot. Classical Georgian style with a parapet running along the front to hide the gulley roofs and chimneys. A steep staircase connected the levels with a half landing large enough to turn a coffin. The handrail was made of pine. Tenants for the new buildings came from outside London. Robert Bell grew up in Watford and was apprenticed to his father. When he married Ann they pooled their resources and hoped that London's streets would be paved with gold. The new building in Paddington Street was just affordable to rent. Plenty of upstairs rooms for the children that they produced.

Robert Bell had help making shoes from his family. His wife might have sewn the uppers together using pig's bristles at the end of the twisted threads. Robert would have gone to the market to buy the leather from a tanner in Leather Lane in London. A long walk especially carrying it rolled up on his back. Upper leather would have been thinner and lighter. It was made from young animals such as calves and kids. The sole leather was much heavier. It was from old cows and bulls and he would watch out that the tan had gone through the skin and not left a layer that could go rotten. That is where the saying "See any green?' comes from. Robert's work was to secure the soles to the uppers. He had a way of pulling the uppers over the lasts so that there would not be wrinkles or pleat at the toe or heels.

The lasts would have a wet layer of leather attached to the base and when they had dried the uppers would be pulled over with a margin around the sides. The outer leather soles would then hold the layers by having lots of wood pegs hammered into them. The pegs were often made from poplar wood because it could be split into thin layers and cut up really small. A good job for children. All the family worked as soon as they were able. Earning enough to buy food was not easy. They went to the church around the corner and got well known for being helpful and making good shoes. Robert could make for men and women, measuring them up in the grand front room of the house. It had the largest fireplace in the house. The workroom was behind.

The cellar was used for cooking and storing the leather and firewood, with the privy in the back yard.

Robert toiled on for the next 30 years with his family. The children learnt the craft and in 1820 when King George 3rd died, Robert also passed on his business to his eldest son. Robert had bad eyesight and his arthritic hands made it impossible to work. His son James had taken a wife and had a family and they shared the rooms over the shop. Robert and his wife died and James tried new ways to sell shoes. Instead of just making to order he made shoes in various styles and size to sell ready made. It was fairly successful sometimes, but other times he was landed with a load of dead stock that just cluttered up his rooms. It happened really badly in 1860 when he was forced into bankruptcy. He and his wife had to move into the Luxborough Work House nearby. Their children went to work for other shoemakers.

Howard de Walden had no problem finding new tenants. The Rudkins had a thriving Sanitary Engineering business and they moved into 4 Paddington Street. One of the first improvements they made was to dig up the basement floor and lay pipes to connect the privy to the new sewer that had been built in Paddington Street. The sewer connected to the one that ran along the stream that had been buried in Marylebone High Street. London in those years was in turmoil. Sewers and then the new underground railway along the Marylebone road were being built. During the winter months there was mud everywhere and when it got warmer there were the smells and flies.

John Rudkin had cast iron drain covers made to go over the inspection pits and was proud to put his name and address on the two that he installed in his home. The wall between the front and back room was demolished to make one larger one. The sanitary engineering business did not need a shop, but his wife wanted to sell secondhand furniture and that needed space. The shop needed a wider pavement in front of the window and so the gap was covered over with red tiles surrounded by white marble. In the middle was a raisable pair of glazed cellar flaps. To make it easy for coal to be delivered to the cellars under the pavement round metal plates were installed. All the neighbours had them too. Charles Dickens lived at the top end of Marylebone High Street for a few years and bought furniture from the Rudkins.

Like so many businesses there were times when trade boomed or didn't. In the 1880s there was a huge housing shortage in London as people flocked there, either from the problems on the continent or because of changing agricultural practices that made people redundant. The Rudkins found they could make easy money by letting out rooms on two of the three floors above the shop. Each floor had a separate family. One made portmanteaus, another umbrellas. To cope with their basic needs another two toilets were installed. One on the half landing above the first floor and another by using part of the back room on the first floor. The room has strange proportions being long and narrow with a very high ceiling and a small window.

The furniture shop eventually was no longer viable and so the Rudkins went into selling wallpaper and paint. Nowadays opposite is a branch of Farrow and Ball who also sell paint and wallpaper.

During World War 2 bombs were dropped on the area. The building did not suffer a direct hit, but the house on the other side of the street on the corner of Marylebone High Street was. In the attics of No 4 There are cracks in the party walls that are about an inch wide. Fortunately they have not increased in size since the war. The glass in the back windows is not perfectly smooth and the sash windows date from when the place was built.

In the 1920s the Howard de Walden Estate sold the freeholds of the houses in Paddington Street between Marylebone High Street and Nottingham Street. Possibly to pay death duties. The Rudkins were able to buy theirs and lived over the shop. The pressure on living accommodation eased as more houses and flats were built. The nearest were the Peabody Buildings just through Grotto Passage where there was also a "ragged school", for poor children.

In 1954 the building came on the market for £12,500. My father had rented a shop in nearby Blandford Street. A couple of years before he had with his business partner bought a long established firm of shoemakers called James Taylor & Son. Space was extremely cramped in Blandford Street and so it was that the business moved to 4 Paddington Street. I remember helping to move things and carrying boxes from one shop to the other as an 8 year old.

After the bombing in London there was a shortage of office space and so my father successfully applied for office user for the upper floors. He used the shop and basement for the business. The first floor was a consulting room and office, and the top floor rear room was a storeroom. It had boxes with old James Taylor stock. Mainly thin pointed toed ladies shoes. Some had diamanté decoration on and many had Louis heels. There was an old washbasin with just a cold tap that was rather elaborate. Everything was dirty and dusty and one of my first jobs was to make a list of it all. The cellars under the pavement were very damp because water would drip down from the arched ceilings. I went to Oxford Street and bought sheets of corrugated clear plastic that I fixed to the walls and ceilings. That helped make it drier so perishable things could be stored there.

James Taylor customers also returned for more shoes for decades and some families for generations. I met customers who told me they had written in their wills that they wished to be buried in their shoes, after all they touched their soles.

When I first saw the building and the surrounding ones the walls were blackened by the soot from coal fires. All the chimneys in winter belched out sulphurous smoke. The air could turn yellow and so thick with smog that it was impossible to see where you were walking. It made me wheezy. The Smokeless Zone act cleaned up the air, and we had a tenant on the top floor called "Clean Walls" and they washed buildings and London became a brighter city. That firm even cleaned up the Houses of Parliament. They grew and moved to larger offices.

As a child in the 50's I sometimes came with my father to the shop. We would take the 13 bus from Golders Green and travel upstairs. I remember a huge empty bomb site used as a vehicle park for army lorries where 55 Baker

Street is now. I think a V2 bomb had demolished the block. It became the M&S head offices and has again been redeveloped. Strange how some older buildings survive much longer than newer ones. 4 Paddington Street is in a conservation area. The old wooden sash windows have been kept and need repainting and are draughty. Secondary glazing has made the rooms warmer and quieter.

I also remember the bakery at the corner of Paddington Street and Nottingham Street. We bought iced buns there for the tea break. In the winter the rooms were heated with paraffin stoves. They smelt and could produce a lot of soot. My father also had an illuminated box sign made. It still hung over the entrance until comparatively recently. Planning regulations have banned them but old ones can be kept. He also installed lots of neon tubes for lighting. They were very good in the work rooms but in later years in the shop they were concealed or changed. In 1972 I saw a rag and bone man going past with his horse and cart. I spotted a round metal light fitting and bought it for two pounds. It still hangs in the front of the shop. For lamp shades I chose white globes because those were the lamps shades on the street lighting at the junction of Baker Street and The Marylebone Road. I often thought if Robert Bell had visited the workshops nowadays the biggest improvement he would have found were the electric lights. So many other things would have been familiar, because most of the shoe construction is by hand.

The fireplaces were boarded over in the floors above the shop and most tenants used night storage or fan heaters. Then in the 1990s I had the covers taken off the fireplaces and they were features. Plenty of soot and dead pigeons were found. In the back half of the basement there is a black range that must have cooked lots of meals.

I enjoyed giving people tours of the workrooms. Peoples eyes would pop out when they came down to the basement and they saw all the walls covered with rows of lasts. Hanging like bats, each was named and numbered. They were made of hornbeam wood with leather fittings. The racks built in my father's time were made of one inch square battens and the lasts lay on them collecting dust. I replaced them with old gas pipes and the pairs of lasts hung over them. We could pack more in and they did not collect so much dust. What Robert Bell did not have was a finishing machine. The firm had a succession of them to grind away surplus leather or rubber. Despite dust bags there was always lots of dust about.

The shop window was in three sections when my father moved in. He had it replaced with one large pane. It was one of the largest plate glass panes in London at the time. The shop faces south and a sun blind was installed. It had the words, "Anatomical Shoemakers" included which sounded very grand or incomprehensible. In latter years it was replaced with a Burgundy coloured one and Bespoke Shoemakers written on it. The sides of the blind had arms that came down fairly low and our sales manager was highly amused when he saw a policeman whose helmet was knocked off. Because the sun would bleach the shoes the glass was covered with a film to reduce it. When first installed it was rather wrinkly.

The seating layout was mainly along the wall facing the shop door. Three green leather benches with two dividing display cabinets between. Useful for people to steady themselves with when they stood up. Facing into the shop were some chairs with red leather seats. I sometimes thought the red ones were for the Lords and the green for the Commoners. Certainly the shop served plenty of both.

The shop counter was close to the door and had the autograph till screwed to it so that a thief could not snatch it away. It was dark wood with a draw that was pulled open to put the cash in. Before pulling the draw one had to write what the transaction was for on a roll. Then pull the draw open and a bell would ring. I liked this because it made me feel as if I was a real shop keeper. As computerisation came in book keepers looked at more advanced tills to make their lives easier, but I resisted them because more and more transactions were by card and not so many by cash.

The shop door had metal handles. Over the years they had been polished so much that the chrome had worn away revealing brass that then shone beautifully.

My father did not sell ready-made shoes, but in 1972 we took over a firm that sold high quality men's shoes called Edward Green. Over the recent years we went on to sell several other sorts of comfort shoes for men and women. The exception were Status shoes to make men 4 centimetres taller. The shoes had to be ordered in bulk from a Northampton factory. They were stored in the attic. The building had a gully roof with two roof spaces. One was easy to reach, but the other had to have a trap door made in the ceiling of what was the office on the top floor. The area had been sealed since it was built in 1790.

The rafters were of different sizes and salvaged from older buildings. Signs of wattle and daube showed and they still had hand-made square nails. Chipboard flooring, electric lighting and racks with Status shoes went in. The original loft had old wooden sides of drinks boxes as flooring with the names of good brands. There is a trap door from the loft onto the roof. The golden ladies on the top of St Marylebone parish church can be seen in one direction and the playground on the roof of the school in Blandford Street the other way.

The old slates moved so much that there were leaks. In 1990 new roof tiles were put on. That was not without problems because the builders did not protect the roof enough when it rained and water flowed onto the files of the tenant on the top floor who was most upset by it.

My father built up a good relationship with the many doctors in the Harley Street area and they referred many patients for footwear. People also heard about the firm from the Yellow Pages and the Quaker magazine "The Friend". The BBC had offices in Marylebone High Street and occasionally we were the subject of programmes. The basement was used as a film set for "The Last of Lindacleer" an anagram for Cinderella." The film company brought in so many vans that they filled up our end of Paddington Street.

During the miners strike in the 1970s Britain was put on a three day week because of a shortage of energy. Making shoes by hand only needed light so lots of oil lamps and even a Tilley lamp were brought in. Despite all these preparations they were never needed. We could see blackouts on the other side of the street, but our power was never lost. Maybe because we were on the circuit of The King Edward VII hospital where the Royal family are treated.

Paddington Street had two way traffic and cars queued outside the shop to turn into Marylebone High Street. People could see our window. Those who found walking difficult could even park. Meters were introduced and my father successfully had a single yellow line installed outside the shop so that ambulances could also find room to stop when they brought patients from hospitals. There was chaos when large lorries or busses parked or try to pass. There would be a lot of hooting. A neighbour who seemed to always be out side on the pavement would shout " Quiet please".

It was a huge relief when a one way system was introduced. Blagdon's the fishmonger was opposite for many years. Old John Blagden used to park his Rolls Royce outside in the 70s but then he downsized to a Mini. As traffic built up traffic wardens were introduced. Blagdon's were often in trouble with their delivery van and would cover number plates to avoid fines. We would watch the daily skirmish as wardens took photos and David Blagdon took photos of them. Our customers also had problems when disabled who could hardly walk were unfairly penalised. I was glad our staff used public transport or bikes. There was a hoist for my bike in the hallway. The ground floor has high ceilings so there is plenty of room to walk below.

Paddington Street Gardens during warmer weather are a huge outdoor restaurant for all the workers at lunchtime. The public conveniences won awards and as we had no ground floor toilets sometimes I sent people there. In the gardens is a statue of a small boy sitting mending one of his shoes. The title is "The crossing sweeper". At one time the streets were full of horse and other mess and the crossing sweep had to keep the crossings clear. Not a pleasant job. This statue is very sweet and was even stolen. Being made of marble it is very heavy and the thieves dropped it out side the Gunmakers pub, breaking off an arm and a leg. The statue was restored to the Garden with and arm and leg. They are weathering nicely to match the rest of the marble.

None of my family or relatives wanted to take on running the business when I felt the time was right to retire at the age of 66. I was glad to find a buyer for the firm but my family kept ownership of the building.

It provides a good pension for what I call my permanent holiday.

Part of the loft floor

Step 10

Boots by bike

In the 1970s several shoemaking firms closed and I was able to either buy them or simply take over their customers. The first one was Kembers who had a shop in Montpelier Street close to Harrods. They made shoes to measure and also retailed very high quality men's shoes made by a Northampton firm called Edward Green. The Kember brothers wanted to retire and I had met them at a meeting of The West End Master Bootmakers Association. They had a lot of prestigious customers and by taking over the lasts the customers came to us. We had an agreement to pay a commission on every successful order and it worked well.

Bob Kochan had a shop and passed his business and some staff to us when his lease expired. He had an NHS contract and did a lot of business with University College Hospital. The Appliance officer, Mrs Richardson was often in contact and she sent many patients to us.

I had my mother's old bike in London with a wicker work basket on the front to put shoes in. We had patients through our NHS contract from many of the London hospitals and I would do rounds usually in the afternoons. At first I used an A-Z street directory to find my way but soon no longer needed it. I had the knowledge. The nearest was Princess Grace Hospital and the furthest St. Bartholomew's (Barts) in the City of London and St Thomas's over Westminster Bridge. I would bring finished boots and shoes and collect orders. Often the Appliances would offer me a cup of tea and I would tell them about my young family and the shop. At Christmas I would bring the Appliance Officers a box of biscuits in the basket on the bike and my old rucksack.

Our shoe repair business got so busy that I found another firm to do some of the work in Shepherds Bush. I would load all the work on me and the bike and cycle over dodging the traffic and going faster than a lot of it. There were only three times when I had collisions. At a big roundabout near Holborn I was between a van and a car and touched the van. The van driver jumped out and accused me of scratching the paintwork. The van had lots of scratches and scrapes so I said, " Which one?" He was trying it on. Another time a car pulled out from the wrong side of the road and I could not avoid hitting it. Luckily I was going slowly and no harm was done. There were countless near misses especially with pedestrians who would step into the road without looking. Oxford Street was the worst place. To reduce the jaywalkers I would cycle along whistling tunes as loudly as I could. Great way to motivate me and kept me amused.

Sometimes I would combine my trips west on my bike and have lunch with an old school friend who worked at Kensington Town Hall. We had known each other since we were 5 and I had been best man at his wedding in 1968. He had done the same job for me in 1975 when I married in Hamburg.

I took over a business in Tottenham Street close to the Middlesex Hospital. Mr Sikora had a shop there and I kept it running for a while with shoemakers working there. Two rooms on the ground floor and a basement for a workshop. I looked up Kelly's Directories to find out who had occupied it in previous years. In the last years of the 1800s it had been the German Working Mens Club. A frequent visitor was Carl Marx who came to London and wrote "Das

Kapital" A book that was a basis for Communism. In the basement was also the toilet and when the time came for me to move out, I took the old wooden loo seat. Carl Marx may have got some of his inspiration sitting on it!

One shoemaker who worked there for a while was a young man called Robert Llewelyn. He lived in a squat in Regents Park and his mother who lived in Bath would phone me to ask after Robert. Robert got good at making and set up his own business. I did not mind because I wanted the number of shoemaking firms to increase. Over time he left shoemaking and went into writing Scripts for a Television series called Red Dwarf. He also played a robot in it called Creighton. The series has run for years and he has been involved with other television programs making far more money than he would ever have done shoemaking.

A shoemaker in Charlotte Street also passed on his shop and business to me. He was Turkish Cypriot and always put orange peel on his electric fire to give the place a nicer smell. I was frequently calling in using the bike but it was not bringing in any orders or business so I did not renew the lease. I then found that he opened another shop round the corner in Windmill Street.

Taking over other firms did increase the number of Bespoke orders. At the peak we had thirteen hundred bespoke orders a year. A combination of NHS and private orders.

Step 11

By Royal Disappointment

It was a typical Tuesday in my shoemaking shop. Customers came for fittings and others phoned asking about our services. I took a call asking if someone would fly out to Saudi Arabia next Friday to measure the King. I thought it could be a hoax. I asked the caller for their number and said I would ring back.

It was no hoax. The Royal Procurement Office was just round the corner in Baker Street above the cinema. Could I bring samples in that afternoon?

The King's son in law, Mr. Fostock, kept me waiting for while before approving the shoes and leather. He asked me to bring in my passport for a visa the following morning. He told me the King liked Italian styles. Could those be made for him? Sure I said but thought "Why go to a British shoemaker for Italian styles?" Thank goodness I knew the editor of The Shoe and Leather News, Alan Cork. He sent me some Italian shoe magazines, but quite a lot of the adverts in it had photos of sexy looking ladies that I thought might upset the customs officials.

The visa stamped in my passport was impressive and I collected the air tickets at the same time. Mr Fostock and I would be travelling together on Saudi Airlines on Friday. Naturally he sat in first class and I was in economy, but in 1979 films were shown on a screen in economy, so he came back to watch it with me. A seven hour flight and it was night when we landed in Riyadh. I was put in a taxi and it drove off through the honking traffic and wild dogs. It was three in the morning local time when we reached the hotel. A porter guided me to a room and I was surprised to see that the bed was dishevelled. Still I was tired and went to sleep. A man got in next to me and said " I am your bodyguard " Well if that is how they do things here I better go with it and went back to sleep. He was gone when I woke up. A note for me said I would not be needed that day. European business people at the breakfast table were surprised by my story. They had waited months for visas. One showed me round the town. We went to the Souks (markets) and saw the jewellery and gold laid out on open stalls. Every couple of hours the people were called to prayer from the minarets. The sound reminded me of air raid sirens. In the market the stallholders would just toss a sheet of muslin over the valuables. They knew the penalties for stealing were a huge deterrent. The week before a thief had had his hands cut off in the market square.

I had a good nights sleep alone and on the Sunday was collected for lunch at Mr Fostock's home. It was pleasant and we went on to the airport for another flight to Jeddah. I sat next to a woman wearing full burka and found it disconcerting when she kept trying to play footsie with me.

The hotel I was sent to was brand new with marble and glass in abundance and I had a huge room with an ensuite that had poorly finished tiling. A car collected me and took me to the palace on the outskirts of town. It had a wall and scruffy looking guards lounging at the gate.

The palace was a large bungalow and I met Mr Fostock sitting on a bench outside. A convoy of Mercedes arrived and men wearing Arab robes got out. We followed them into a large living room with leather settees. The King turned on the television. When it finished the King waved me over and with Mr Fostock interpreting ordered 14 pairs of shoes with leather belts to match. He chose four styles from the magazines in various colours. On the plane I had checked for mens styles so that he could skip the pages of sexy looking ladies, in case that distracted him.

It was time for dinner. Two huge Arabs with turbans stood in the doorway. One held a bowl of water and soap for us to wash our hands. The other had individual hand towels for us. In the dining room the table had been laid for twelve but we were only six. There was a beautifully embroidered table cloth matching chair seats, covered in clear plastic for protection. The cut crystal wine glasses were filled with water. I had been told that when the King finished eating everyone else did. I dined well and the King would grin at me but not say a word, except through Mr Fostock.

Foot drawings and measurements were taken on the marble hall floor because the paper sank into the thick pile carpet. It occurred to me that here I was of Jewish origin, a Quaker and currently chairman of the Northwood Council of Churches, kneeling in front of The king of Saudi Arabia. A fairy tale. The phrase "Speak truth to Power" came to mind. Through Mr Fostock he asked what I would do with the rest of the evening. I said I have no money. I was given a couple of hundred US dollars. The King then went to be shaved by the barber, presumably before going on to his harem.

Quite glad to have a British Airways flight home. I asked if I could go forward to the pilot and my wish was granted. That wouldn't happen nowadays because of security concerns. It was wonderful to see the River Nile and the green fields alongside carving a path across the desert. The King had asked for some of the shoes to be ready in a fortnight. Normal delivery was three months with fittings to check before completion.

Four pairs of lasts were made and everything given priority. The first batch went to the office in Baker Street and while we waited for news we started on the next shoes. A few days later the first ones returned. They were too big at the back. Adjustments were made to the lasts and the next batch went out only to be returned, too tight over the insteps. I asked Mr Fostock if we could do it our way with just one pair being sent out in a fitting stage without soles. He agreed but then months passed with no news. Eventually I found out that they could not present the King with just one pair of unfinished shoes. They cancelled the remainder of the order and said we could keep the deposit. It taught me to insist, whoever the customer was, that working our way was in their best interest. No doubt other shoemakers had tried, including Italian ones and could call themselves "By Royal Disappointment "

The shoes were sold off in the Sales. I had one pair remade for me. They were light brown glacé kid, elastic under instep with dark brown piping. My wife called them gigolo shoes.

Step 12

Rotary Emblem and More Initials on Toes

Customers sometimes asked for their initials to be punched into the toe caps of their shoes. Most often it was on mens brogue style and showed they were bespoke.

I was invited by a customer to join the Rotary club of St Marylebone in 1983. The round Rotary logo could be found on lots of items such as belt buckles, cuff links, shirts and ties. I had a black calf pair of full brogue shoes made for myself with the logo on the toes caps. I still wear them to club meetings. A regular customer from Hull was also in Rotary and when he saw mine ordered a pair in dark brown.

Apart from customers who had initials on the toe caps, some had other designs. One had teddy bears and another Scottie dogs. The Royal School of Needlework would send customers to us. Ladies had stitched designs onto the fronts of tapestry slippers and wanted them then made up as presents for their loved ones. Usually for Christmas and it could be a struggle to get them done in time. The most memorable design was of a King Charles Cavalier spaniel in light brown with its ears flying wide. We had a similar looking dog at that time, but I didn't have a pair of slippers made for myself like that.

A vicar who knew he would be getting lots of money for his services in bereavement, asked me how many shoes I had. I said a pair for every day of the week so I could wear them in rotation. That way the perspiration dried out and did not rot the leather. He ordered five pairs of black Oxford cap calf shoes. One for Monday to Friday. He asked me, "How can I tell them apart?"

I remembered a customer who also had lots of identical styled shoes.

"We put little brass nails underneath into the waist of the shoes in the shape of numbers. Eventually he got to 33"

Being a cleric he said,

" Let's do them with Roman numerals ".

"Excellent choice " I said.

He ordered another pair of black Oxford cap shoes with grippy Vibram soles for funerals. He had been at a funeral in Kensal Rise just after it had rained making the ground very slippery. The edge of the grave was edged with green artificial grass and a drunken grave digger had lurched towards the hole and grabbed the vicar's hand and down they both went smashing through the coffin. The mourning family were greatly distressed and it was not easy to climb out. The grippy soled shoes might save the day another time.

Step 13

Factory Doctor

My brother trained as a doctor of medicine in Leeds and suggested to me that it could be helpful to the business if we had a factory doctor. Westminster Hospital sent a rather portly patient who had flat feet, and he happened to be a General Practitioner with a surgery next to the Wallace Collection. I asked him if he could be our factory doctor and he was delighted to accept my request. He would come every autumn to give the staff anti flu injections. This was done in the rear workshop and if some did not want to be injected that was ok. He also did anti hay fever ones. It was so helpful when staff could not see their own doctors quickly they could phone and pop round to see him. The firm benefitted too because they did not have to take much time off. Our last maker, Harry, called in sick one day. He lived in Hampstead and so I phoned the good doctor and told him.

"Where does he live?"

I gave him the address.

"Oh that is on my way home. I will call in this evening"

To my relief the next day Harry could come in. The doctor had sorted his back out so quickly.

In payment he had a pair of shoes made for him each year. Eventually he had more shoes than he needed so his son and his wife had some. Our Sales manager David Worrell had his life saved by the doctor. David had felt unwell and gone to see his own GP who said come back in a week. David felt very bad when he arrived next morning so I sent him round to our doctor. He examined him and called an ambulance to take him to St Mary's Hospital in Paddington. He was operated on the same day with a stent put in his heart. Amazingly he was back at work after a week. David was a very popular man with a lot of customers because of his cheerful character. Maybe because of that customers would order more than one pair at a time. When the good doctor reached the age when NHS doctors are told to retire, he continued to practice from a basement room below an estate agent nearby. As the years went on he was delighted to see patients even though they were non NHS and he had to charge them. I am sure he used his discretion and we continued paying with shoes and shoe repairs. Sadly the good doctor died at the age of 90. For a time before he died he was in a nearby hospital and I would visit him. He said his greatest enjoyment was being able to help people. I did not manage to find a replacement Factory doctor before I sold the business.

Step 14

Oak Bark Rescue

Bakers tannery of Colton, South Devon have been supplying James Taylor & Son since it was just James Taylor in the 1880s. Bakers have been using the same buildings and pits on a site that go back to Roman times. Oak bark has been used because the tannin in it kills bacteria that would otherwise rot the leather. They tanned the thicker leather used for shoe soles and stiffeners. It would take about a year to tan the leather as it was soaked for some weeks in one pit and then moved on to another pit with a higher concentration of oak bark. When the tannin had been absorbed right through to the middle of the hide it would be ready to be taken out of the pit, it would be rolled and finished, ready for use. There is a saying, "See any green" and if you did then the leather was not fully tanned and when used would soon break down.

Another market for them was saddlery. Old Mr Baker would come to London four times a year to visit shoemakers and take orders. He wore an old gaberdine mac and would always say.

"Have a cigarette".

"No thanks" I would say.

"I do not smoke"

For years he had his grandson in tow and then eventually the grandson took over. I went to visit the tannery a few times and enjoyed being shown round. I once bought a pair of fur lined mitts at the tannery shop to use on my bike.

One day I was told that they were facing closure. Bakers could not find any more oak bark. The woods they had sourced it from had run out of oak, because it had not been planted in recent years. I phoned my old colleagues in the Forestry Commission and told them how much income they could get for something that was usually wasted. That had the desired effect. The New Forest fell and sell stands of oak trees and the bark had been stripped off and left to rot. Instead it was collected and sent to Bakers tannery. The tannery is still running using British hides and oak bark.

Marylebone has had a lot of Street trees planted over the years and l know the Westminster tree Officer. He told me about a scheme to sponsor trees to be planted in memory of a person.

Both of Frank Taylor's daughters had died so I sponsored two trees to be planted. One close to where the shop had been at 82 Great Portland Street and the other in Weymouth Street close to Paddington Street. They both had plaques explaining why, inserted in the pavement.

The St Marylebone Rotary club also sponsored a tree to be planted in Paddington Street Gardens at my suggestion. It was a Medlar tree and is a fairly rare species. The fruit have to be treated before they can be eaten.

Close to the shop in the High Street is a notable Elm tree that has survived the elm disease because it is isolated by buildings. The beetles that spread the disease in the 1970s did not find it. It is higher than the three storey buildings and the branches reach over the road. Lights are put on them at Christmas.

Step 15

Pink Elephant Shoes

Most customers just wanted black or brown leather shoes and it was great when something different was ordered. In the mid 1970s an accountant who worked near by ordered platform soled ankle boots with high chunky heels in pink elephant skin. Have you ever seen a pink elephant? Mr Wilson our pattern cutter had been with the firm since 1932 and knew of a firm in South London called R. and A. Konstamm who dealt in exotic skins. I phoned and yes they had pink elephant, so Mr Wilson and I went by train to see it and then buy some. Leather is sold by the square foot and elephant skin has a pattern on in like large finger prints. Mr Wilson needed to see that the skin would be soft and subtle to work with. The leather chosen was from the ears.

The boots looked wonderful when they were finished and I know what an accountant in the pink looks like.

Several customers came with uppers they had stitched at the Royal School of needlework to make into slippers for their husbands. The most amazing was of a King Charles Cavalier spaniel with it's ears flying outwards.

Another had shot an ostrich and had it's skin tanned in South Africa. He had shoes and a briefcase made from it. Fairly often we had Nigerian customers who wanted shoes made of crocodile. I was tempted to say "Shoot your own". One was a chief who had one leg half an inch shorter than the other. The shoes had to be made with a concealed raise to balance him. He would order several pairs at a time and pay us thousands of pounds in cash. I would, after he left, jump on my bike and take it to the bank. Over the years we made shoes and boots with other materials. Python, stingray, salmon skin, canvas and silk.

I also made shoes for dogs twice. The first was for a girl friend's dog that had arthritis in it's feet. The other was for the daughter of the St Marylebone vicar. The pug dog would pull and slide on it's feet so much that the pads would bleed.

People from the Museum of London brought in shoes from a dig by the Thames that they dated from 1200. They were intrigued to learn from me that they had been made inside out. The seams holding the uppers together were inside. The shoes would have been soaked to make them soft and pliable after they were sewn and them a stick poked into the toe and pulled round. Called a "Turn shoe". Ballet shoes are still made that way. The medieval shoes had very long pointed toes that were stuffed with moss.

Step 16

West End Master Bootmakers Terms of Business

I had been introduced to this august organisation by Ruby Hiatt who used the first floor room to host meetings. The West End Master Bootmakers Association had been founded in 1908 when there were 300 bespoke shoemakers, just in the West End of London. The masters wanted to have agreements on how much to pay outworkers on piece work. The idea was that firms would not poach staff from other firms by offering higher rates of pay to come and work for them. It was a Trade Association and had a President and Honorary Secretary. In the early 1970s it was run by a credit rating organisation who checked if customers were of good standing. That way when orders were placed by people who had not made a deposit the shoemaker could know that they were likely to be paid. Some customers only paid their bills at the end of a year. Firms sent out bills asking to be respectfully paid. They traded on overdrafts and were slow paying their bills.

The President of the Association was Eric Lobb, of the firm that made shoes for the Royal Family. As the years went by the secretary retired and I took the job on.

Initially we met at the Royal Overseas club in Park Place and had tea in a room over looking Green Park. In later years we met at the Cavendish Hotel in Jermyn Street in the lounge. With only a handful of members we could sit around a coffee table and sip our tea as we went through an agenda. There I learnt how each firm was fairing. All the others made mostly for men because men will generally pay more for shoes and they do not have higher heels and so many more styles. They sent representatives abroad twice a year to take orders or do fittings and would stay in a prominent hotel and see clients by appointment. I was not keen on the idea of sitting in a hotel room for hours so I never copied them.

We only met once or twice a year when we had a social meeting. There was a boat trip with a buffet on the Thames or meals in restaurants. There were only eight members when I took over and the number of firms went down in the forty years I was involved. The Lobbs sometimes invited me to the Royal Warrant holders dinners that were held in Grosvenor House on Park Lane. At one dinner I met a neighbour from the basement of 6 Paddington Street. He held a warrant for belt making. Ronnie was very helpful for parts that we did not have. Coloured eyelets in particular, because one had to order a thousand at a time and only a score were needed at any one time.

Some of the members passed on a brilliant idea to help cash flow that they had learnt from Savile Row tailors. When they took a bespoke order they asked for a substantial deposit and the balance on completion, or offered a small discount if customers paid in full with the order. We tried it out and found that most customers were quite happy to pay in full even though we told them that they would not get their shoes for several months. Life got so much better. We traded without an overdraft and could get discounts from suppliers for prompt payment. We applied the idea to shoe repairs and ready made shoes that we would order in. Customers generally would come in very promptly when we let them know shoes were ready, and we did not have shoes waiting taking up precious space in the shop.

Eric Lobb

Step 17

I Am – a Last

The story starts with a piece of ash in the soil. Beech mast fell and one germinated and absorbed the ash over time into a fine beech tree. The trunk was tall, straight and knot free. The time came for it to be felled and cut into foot long lengths. These were then split into wedges and left to dry before being taken to a factory to be put on lathes and made into lasts for making bespoke shoes on. I am a right size 8 shoe last and of course have a fellow left. We were bought by a shoemaker in London who wanted stock lasts to make shoes on for his wellheeled customers.

My fellow last and I were kept in a sack for a time until a customer with size 8 feet ordered a classic Oxford cap pair of shoes. We were taken and placed on the paper with the drawings of his feet. The last fitter then added pieces of mellowed leather that had been skived thin at the sides under the arches, because the customer was rather flat footed. We were then rasped and shaped to produce a squarer toe shape, which was what the customer wanted. Quite a game to make us look a pair again. When the last fitter thought the work on us was finished, we were passed on to the pattern cutter. A line was drawn from the top of my cone to the middle of the toe and another down the centre of the back of the heel. Paper was then pushed against me and trimmed to make the standard pattern, that was used to make all the parts, vamp, quarters, caps and linings.

We could rest on a shelf while the patterns were used for cutting the upper leather and then the parts were sewn together to make the uppers or tops of the shoes. Our services came when the shoemaker blocked the wet leather insole on our base and then pulled the uppers over us. Small lasting nails were used to secure the uppers to the insoles. They stood out making us look a bit like hedgehogs in reverse. The shoemaker checked that the uppers were on properly. The toe caps looked a pair, the sides tightly pulled against our sides. We had been hammered a fair bit as the stiffeners and toe puffs were smoothed and that was no hardship as our wood was hard.

The shoemaker then sewed in a welt around the edge of our base, pulling the lasting nails out as the welt held the upper to the insole. He could not at that stage see the holes left where the nails had been. Those holes were what was to eventually wear me out. The leather soles were then stitched to the welts and well hammered again against my base to ensure they would not stretch or squeak. Customers do not like noisy shoes. The uppers had been firmly pulled down on me and the time came for the shoes to come off. A block of wood had been sawn in my cone and held in with a screw. This was undone and the cone could be pulled out. Then the hard part, pulling the rest of me out of the shoe. The last hook went onto a hole near the heel at the side and the shoemaker pulled with his fingers against the sides of the shoes. Plenty of broken finger nails. With a clatter on the floor, I was free. My block was replaced and I could go and rest with my fellow.

The shoes returned to be resoled on me. I was pushed back in with a strong metal shoe horn. That way the shoes would have all the wear creases smoothed out. While the old thin soles with holes were removed and the new ones stitched to the welts we learnt where the shoes had been. The customer was a High Court judge. Horrible people had appeared before him. He said to the shoemaker, "I hope your son never appears before me"

I was next taken from our rack to be used as templates for shoe trees and taken to the last makers hanging over bicycle handle bars to Alans, the tree makers in Gosforth Street, close to Great Portland Street. There was a green painted door between houses. The door would be opened by Charlie or Dave. If it was Dave he would say "Oh no not you again" and take us through a passage with large planks of beech wood stored over head. There I was put into Gilman laths next to blocks of wood that were shaped just like us. A clever machine to make clones. These blocks then were cut and hollowed to make into shoe trees that would keep the shoes crease free.

The Judge must have died because the next time we were used the last fitter changed the leather fittings and made our toes shape rounder. A different name was written on me. I went to the pattern cutter again and this time walking boots were designed on the standard pattern. The boots had to have several fittings before they satisfied the customer and each time more nails were driven into me and pulled out. It is around the toes where they are closest because that is where the leather pleats and has to be stretched out to make a smooth edge. This customer must have been young because every year or so different styles of shoes were made. I was never needed to be copied for shoe trees, but a time came when I went again to the last makers. They were in a back yard down the private ally again. Rather spooky with sawdust piled high in sacks and big planks stored under the ceiling. I was put on the copying lathe and a pair of lasts cloned. So many pairs of boots and shoes had been made that all the nail holes had joined up to produce a big groove. No good for making more shoes on me any more.

I was chucked on a heap with other old lasts and taken to be burnt in a wood burning stove. That's life. My ashes were dumped in a garden and some beech mast fell on me. One germinated and you know the rest of the story. It's everlasting.

Step 18

Interruptions

The story of most of my working life. I would make a list of what I needed to do each morning as I travelled into London on the train. It was rare that I could get it all done, because of interruptions. I sometimes felt I was like Figaro. Figaro, here, there and everywhere. Running a bespoke shoe-shop with a staff of a dozen, being a shopkeeper, and having to wear a lot of hats, I found the best relaxation was juggling, because that is what I did all day. When I was fifty I enrolled on a juggling evening course, run by a remarkable man who had wonderful skills. He called himself Colonel Custard and could ride a unicycle and juggle apples that he ate as he went, and do a load of other amazing feats. Being middle aged it took me a term to learn to juggle three balls, then a year to be able to juggle clubs, and another year to pass the clubs to another juggler in rows. Pop music was played so that there was a beat to give timing. The clubs flying through the air looked so spectacular and the evenings passed all too quickly.

The phone was the greatest source of interruptions because callers wanted immediate answers. The most frequent was how much is it to have shoes made? Put like that money was the main interest, not the shoes. Sometimes it was from foreigners who would say "I want to make shoes" and that was harder to answer because really they wanted to know about having shoes made for them. Another was "When will my shoes be ready?" The longer they talked the longer they would have to wait. We did not have mobile or cordless phones so when I was in the basement workshop once our German receptionist at that time told my wife "She would put her down" My wife survived.

It was hard to offer a while-you-wait service with repairs or foot supports because there would be interruptions so sometimes I invited customers to come and watch as the work was done. They would come with me into the workshop and see all the other work, tools and leather and be almost overwhelmed by it. That overcame their possible impatience. There was a nuisance caller who would frequently phone and ask "Is your tongue hanging out?" What was that all about? It went on for weeks. We thought we recognised his voice and the game ended when we said "Yes Mr. Smith."

Of course my all time interruption was on my honeymoon when we reached a cottage in the Schleswig-Holstein countryside. The front door had been decorated with an arch of roses, rather romantically. By 9 o'clock we were ready for our nuptial bed, when there was a knock on the door and a shrill voice of the neighbour called out "Am I disturbing you?"

Not half! I thought. But my dear new wife said, "Do come in" and we chatted with her for half an hour. Whether she got the hint to go I don't know, but when she did we could continue to consummate our marriage.

An untidy desk is better than an
empty mind

Step 19

Kinky Callipers

Most of the shoes that we made for people were because they needed them but of course there were some who just liked and wanted handmade-to-measure shoes in the styles they wanted. We also supplied hospitals with callipers and leg irons that slotted into the shoes with a socket in the heel. Often it was people who had no strength in the ankle and knee joints and needed supporting so they could stand. Sometimes caused by polio or other diseases. In the mid 1990s people started asking for sockets to be fitted into shoes and boots so that they could fit callipers into them. Some people wanted full-length callipers that reached right up to the crutch and had complicated knee joints. These were expensive and I wondered why they ordered them. In my innocence I did not know about sexual bondage and so I asked them to sign a disclaimer saying that the firm would not be liable for any injury they might do to themselves wearing them. Some customers wanted them for both legs and others wanted callipers that were made to go into boots with cork lifts to make one leg higher than the other. That could easily give back trouble and so I was even more keen that they signed that they would not sue the firm for that.

One customer ordered boots with cork raises in both and full-length callipers and did not baulk at the price when I quoted it. Over six thousand pounds. He paid in full with a discount and we went ahead. He came for two fittings before they were finished and then again when they were completed. He did not appear particularly excited and in the shop we put the former hospital screen around him so that he could have some privacy. I had helped him put the callipers and boots on and left him for a few moments when I heard a sort of rasping heavy deep breathing. I looked round the corner of the screen and saw that he had collapsed on the bench. I went over to give him first-aid. Mainly to keep his airway open. Being a heavy man I could not lift him onto the floor to put him into a recovery position. At the same time I asked Fiona Campbell our designer, who was serving a customer in the next bench to phone an ambulance. Within a few minutes and ambulance man was there who had come in a car. He was able to assess that a customer had had a heart attack and did artificial respiration. An ambulance came with a resuscitator and this was attached to our customer and we heard it say stand back, "shocking". It took about half an hour before they were able to ensure that our customer was fit to go on a stretcher to the ambulance. There were bits of plastic bags all over the shop floor and it looked like some sort of battlefield. We were told that he would be taken to the Accident and Emergency at University College Hospital.

Next day I phoned the hospital to be told that he'd been transferred to the National Heart hospital in Westmorland Street which is very close to the shop. I went round there and was able to go up to the ward. There were only six beds with masses of machinery around each one. Our customer was still unconscious but on my first-aid course I have learnt that peoples' hearing is often still able to function even when they are unconscious. I spoke a few words to him and then left. The next day I returned to the hospital and the day after but he was always unconscious. My family and I went on holiday for a week and when I phoned up the hospital again on our return learnt that he had been discharged and was home. I was quite surprised to learn that. A few weeks later the University College Hospital Casualty Department phoned to ask if the callipers and boots could be collected as they were taking up a lot of room. I agreed to collect them and cycled round. I felt very self-conscious as I cycled along the Marylebone Road with these callipers sticking out on each side of my bicycle on the carrier. I phoned up the customer and told him I had them and he said he didn't want them and we could keep them even though he had paid in full for them. For many years we used them as display models for the steady stream of people who still seem to want to order them even though they didn't need them.

Step 20

Museum

A museum about a person should be set up by others, just like public relations. It is immodest to think of creating one for yourself and yet I think of the ones I have visited. In St Paul's Cathedral in London there is a tribute to the architect Sir Christopher Wren and it reads, "For my monument, look around you". The biggest Museum I have ever visited was in Dearborn, Michigan, USA. It was the Henry Ford Museum. The whole town was dedicated to him. Henry Ford Hospital, Henry Ford High School, Henry Ford this that and you name it. The museum covered several acres and had a full size steam train running round. There were huge buildings housing every sort of airplane, car, bus, locomotive and a section dedicated to his friend Edison who was sponsored by Henry Ford to find an electric element that could be used in vehicle headlights. Edison tried over a thousand different filaments and each failure was marked off as a success that that was not the one, until he came to tungsten which he patented. The museum even had a collection of houses that famous people had lived in. Henry Ford was born to poor Irish parents who emigrated to the USA. He died in a Mansion with three sorts of electric power. Hydro-electric, a steam generator and back up batteries. There was a massive flood as he died and everything failed. He was born in candlelight and died in candlelight.

In Baker Street, London there is a Museum to a fictitious person. Sherlock Holmes. It is in a Georgian town house, rather like the one I am a part owner of in Paddington Street, not far away. Conan Doyle the author of Sherlock Holmes does not have a museum dedicated to him as far as I know, but that character caught the imagination of many people.

I have a vey long lifeline up the middle of my left hand and it inspires me to aim to live for 150 years. Hopefully enjoying living in every respect. To do that I will have to have a good source of income. Having written a diary about my life as a shoe manufacturer, forester, Rotarian and Quaker, I wonder if the saying "keep a diary and one day it will keep you" could come true. Samuel Pepys managed.

Dreaming on, could I write a book that would be used for television with repeats bringing income.

Someone else could then use elements of my life to make museums.

I always thought I ran a living Museum having a business making shoes in this day and age by hand for individual customers. No mass production like Henry Ford, or built in obsolescence. Having an NHS contract for a large part of my working life enabled people who needed footwear to have them free. So lovely to see Countesses and char ladies sitting together and comparing their feet. Lords leaping in joy when they could dance without pain, and down and outs walking cheerfully.

The building in Paddington Street is still partly owned by me. Like the Sherlock Holmes museum there is a staircase from the basement to the third floor. It does not lend itself to crowds.

The basement has the workshop and leather store that gives the building the aroma of oak bark tanned leather. The ground floor has the shop with displays of model shoes and swatches of upper leather that customers choose from. There is another workshop behind where the shoe uppers are made using sewing machines. The first floor was my father's office and he had a big Globe Wernicke bookcase with hundreds of different miniature shoes. Those rooms could be a Cobblers cafe. Cobblers repaired shoes, but shoemakers were called snobs, because they would not lower themselves to work on dirty repairs.

The two floors above have been converted to one bedroom flats, but could have some of my diaries on display. Reading them again I realised that often I was having to solve problems with shoes. As the years went on l found ways to solve recurring ones. When shoes creased a hot air gun would quickly shrink the leather. Sometimes when shoes slipped at the back just doing the shoe laces in another way did the trick.

A blue plaque on the wall would be wonderful. Marylebone is full of them to people like Beaufort who devised the Wind Force Scale, or Simon Bolivar who liberated huge areas of South America from Spain. That plaque is on a house in Duke Street near the Wallace Collection.

The loft in Paddington Street is floored with wooden parts from wine crates. It was put down in the 1950s and could be reused as a wall covering. In the loft are old electrical appliances. A Pye television made in Cambridge, a radio made in Hendon, a tape recorder Made in England and Primus stoves that were once the way the building was heated. They made a bad smell however much the wicks were trimmed.

I am glad I could help fund new benches in Amersham Meeting House when I sold my business. They were built by John Dalton Banks using Douglas fir bought from a saw mill in the New Forest. 40 years previously I had planted Douglas fir and returned to see some of them felled for saw logs. Wishful thinking to imagine that I had been involved in growing the timber that I sometimes sit on.

As the tree warden for Amersham I have got trees planted around the town. Ok, most in my road where there are quite a variety. Cherries, laburnum, may, and ginkgo. They look especially good in the spring and autumn.

My latest project has been to plant an Open orchard at Jordans with a vista to a notable oak that reminds me of Christopher Wren's memorial. "Just look around."

Step 21

Passing It On

My mind immediately goes to football, as the final of the World Cup is being played out between Croatia and France as I write this. The ball is being passed between the players, but the really serious passing on was when I wanted to sell my business and see it continue. So many small firms just fold up when the driving force leaves. I was told only ten percent of small businesses continue so I was glad to find a buyer even though his objectives differed from mine. Making a profit was not top of my list, but they were his. As a result he replaced many of my better paid skilled staff with trainees. Whilst delivery times for bespoke shoes lengthened, profitability improved. After eighteen months of my three year contract to work part time for the firm I was dismissed. An industrial tribunal ruled it was unfair and awarded me compensation. A consequence of passing it on left a sour taste, but my consolation was that I was the landlord and could, with the help of an agent raise the rent to market value.

My knowledge as an orthopaedic shoe man has not stopped me passing on suggestions to people who I meet. Such as if I see people limping then I can explain how their shoes can be modified to balance them and reduce back ache. It is a delicate balance not to offend so I do not accost strangers. We all have acquired knowledge and it is easy to pass it on when not asked and appear too clever. Still I do enjoy going out as a volunteer with the Chiltern Society and being in work parties. It is the outdoor gym and we can see the results of pulling up ragwort, removing strangling plastic tree guards, or cutting down invasive holly in beech woods.

The real passing on is inheritance. My ancestors have done it over the generations and yet I know so little about so many of them. In our dining room there are portraits of my mother's great great grandparents. I know their names and dates, but nothing else. What traditions, mannerisms, quirks or even skills like music or humour have I had passed to me? Similarly when I die my children and grandchildren will inherit my genes and possibly my worldly goods, but will they enjoy and use things, in what I would call a wise way.

I think of the song Paul Robeson sang " That Old man river, that old man river,

He must know somethin, he don't say nothin, he just goes rolling along.

The last Christmas tree.

Step 22

30 Ways to Walk Cheerfully

1. Go barefoot on warm sand. For many that is what can happen on holiday by the sea side leaving footprints. That can be the freest and loveliest way to walk and be cheerful.

2. When your toes are free that is when your feet are most comfortable and so it follows that footwear that is foot shaped and does not squeeze the toes is likely to be most comfortable. You don't even know you have got shoes on!

3. When walking one should walk heel to toe with the feet the equivalent of five to one on a clock. The heel comes down first and the foot rolls over at the joint and steps off at the toe. Definitely not flat down.

4. Closed toed footwear should be up to an inch longer than the longest toe so that it will not push against the shoe at toe off. Repeatedly pushing against the shoes makes the joints of the toes give way and form bunions on the sides of big toes and hammer toes on the others. In time they lead to grief.

5. Styles of footwear that are likely to be more comfortable hold the foot back so the toes are clear of the front. Usually done with laces, straps or come high up the instep, like clogs.

6.   Laces are best tied up to keep the feet back but they easily can open again. Flat laces are better, but round laces look neater. The knotted bow can be tied a second time on one side so they stay knotted but are easy to pull open.

7.   There are elasticated laces that can be permanently tied up. They make life for mothers of children a lot more cheerful.

8.   Some people have pain in the ball of the foot and this can be cured with a pad just behind the painful area. The result is often instant.

9.   Some people have feet that pronate inwards and there are several ways to help straighten the ankles. Pads, stiffeners, wedges and extended heels are devices that shoemakers use. Again the result can rapidly help people to walk cheerfully.

10.   A tip often given to those with swollen ankles and legs that helped was to sit with the feet flat on the floor and keeping the heel in contact with the ground to raise the front of the foot up and down. The blood supply in the legs is pushed round by the valves in the calf muscles and the swelling is reduced. Very useful when sitting for a long time and footwear gets tight. Do some peddling and when you get tired of it have a rest, but then repeat.

11.   Hip and knee joints take a lot of hammering in a lifetime, so it is good to have shock absorbing heels to reduce the wear on the joints and avoid having surgery. Steel heels on hard pavements are so likely to cause the problems so avoid shoes which you can

hear clicking on the ground. Sometimes it is hard plastic and those can be as bad as steel.

12.   Walking boots are often well designed and have padded collars around the ankles, but avoid doing up the top hooks if you find the they rub.

13.   To avoid blisters in walking boots wear two pairs of thin socks. They insulate the feet and can rub against each other instead of your feet.

14.   You can walk cheerfully in high heels if your feet are held back and your toes are not cramped. Straps and open toed styles are likely to be comfortable. The traditional high heeled court shoe is the cause of a lot of grief.

15.   Some people have back ache because one leg is longer than the other but they are not aware of it. The moment the heel is raised the pain can disappear and so does any limp.

16.   In hot weather it is best to have plenty of air around the feet so perspiration can evaporate. Sandals are the style but there are jobs that insist on shoes so a way to cool the shoes is to punch holes in the uppers in the waist under the arches. The holes are not obvious and air is drawn in and out at every step air conditioning the shoes.

17.   Leather shoes are more likely to be cool because they can absorb perspiration. They often cost more than other materials but if they are made to be repaired the shoes can last decades.

18. The cheeky way to walk more cheerfully is to use a bike. It saves wear and tear on your shoes and is faster.

19. However using a car does the same but the right shoe sole can get worn out on the accelerator.

20. In the winter the ground can get icy so wear shoes that have a good tread and not smooth or a fall can be very painful.

21. When you are walking cheerfully you are not aware of things on your feet and you can enjoy looking up and at your surroundings.

22. When climbing stairs count the number of steps. That takes your mind off the effort of climbing the stairs.

23. Have shoes for all seasons if you can afford them. They are your contact with the world so a worth while investment.

24. Keep your toenails trimmed and that way they will not touch the ends of your shoes.

25. Shoes are good for your mentality and can make you very happy to such an extent that some will wear shoes that physically hurt them and they say "exquisite pain" There are some high heeled mens shoes to help those who want to be taller sometimes to be nearer a girlfriend.

26. Footwear is now an item of fashion for many and so sales are greatly increased as some want the latest and are not interested in having repairs.

27.   Old shoes are like old friends. They have moulded to your sole shape. Watch out that the sides have not got pushed over and can still support the ankles. Usually shoes wear out two heels to one set of soles. Well that is if they are repairable.

28.   I put my left shoe on first, then I know the next one will be right. Please excuse the pun.

29.   Shoe horns can be made of real cow horn, steel, plastic or wood. They make putting some shoes on much easier and save the backs of the shoes being trodden down. Boot jacks make it easier to take them off.

30.   Those with leather shoes will take a pride in having them shiny and polish them. Those with suede shoes can see how to keep them clean by seeing my video https://youtu.be/Dv1Y6_QalWM

Short Autobiography

Peter Schweiger

Born 1945 in Hampstead to refugees from Nazi Germany. They met in the Wye Valley at a settlement run by two Quaker ladies, and came to terms with the awful events that happened to their parents in WW2. They gave up the Jewish religion and joined Quakers taking my brother and myself to the children's class at Golders Green Quaker Meeting.

I was rather average at school in everything and had a wide interest in many things. I bought my first camera with sixpences that I saved up from my pocket money. It was a Kodak Brownie Reflex that was used hanging on my neck and I would look down at a lens/screen on my tummy. That way I could see the subject. It took black and white photos and used roll film that was taken to a chemist for developing and printing.

My parents insisted in keeping me at school until I was 18 and I had A level in Geography and Economics. Most of my school year went on to university, but I was fed up with exams. Instead I worked in my father's London shop for six months where shoes were handmade to measure.

I successfully applied to be trained as a forester with the Forestry Commission. There were four thousand applicants for forty places. It involved a two year slog on piece work in Hampshire and then another couple of years at Gwydyr Forester training school in North Wales with just a dozen in my year. Almost no jobs were available with the Forestry

Commission when the course ended, so I worked for a year as a tractor driver / chainsaw operator with the London Borough of Hillingdon, and failed to get the foresters job with them when the previous one retired. They said I was too commercially minded because I suggested running the thousand acres in a similar way to how the Windsor Estates are run. They sold as much produce as possible from the woods to raise income.

My father had died and his business partner took me on. Back in the London bespoke shoemaking firm, I learnt as much about the practical side of shoemaking before she retired and at the age of 26 took over the management. I was rather daunted by the task of running a staff of 12 older people, having an NHS contract to supply hospital patients, and premises to maintain with tenants on the upper floors. There was a lot of contact with customers, some of whom had links with the firm going back four generations. Notable people were customers, including the former MP for Amersham, Sir Ian Gilmour, and Peter Lewis, grandson of John Lewis.

I had a trip for a weekend to Saudi Arabia to measure up the man who then became King.

I sold the business in 2011 and it is still operating. My family and I are the landlords, so I keep an eye on it, or a toe in the door. There is a good boost to my state pension and we enjoy travelling. I always have taken a camera with me and often feel the urge to take a photo. In more recent years I have been using an I pad because it is so simple and you get what you see on a moderately large screen.

I married Angelica from Hamburg in 1975 and we have Michael and Jenny. Jenny married Dave in 2005 and so we now have grandchildren. William and Holly who take up my wife's time two days a week. I am a Quaker and responsible for the maintenance of six Meeting Houses in the Chiltern area. I am also a past president and secretary of St Marylebone Rotary club and attend regularly.

At least twice a month I volunteer to do woodland work with the Chiltern Society. A Royal Forestry Society member and also in U3A. We have quite a large garden and it is just as well I am retired to have time to enjoy it all.

He was a simple man

His philosophy of life

just two words.

Enjoy it.

To make it even simpler

Enjoy

Then help others To Enjoy.

My last day as owner with the team

Peter's Diary

When the Daily Telegraph printed an article about a court case I had been called to I resolved to try and keep a diary of everyday happenings to me. It will aid my memory and may form the basis of a book one day. Written mainly going to and from work on the train.

Bookie to pay £5,500 to buy ex-wife shoes

A BOOKMAKER was ordered by a High Court judge yesterday to foot the £5,500 bill for new shoes for his ex-wife for the next 10 years.

- The £5,500 for special sandals, shoes and knee-length boots is part of the £27,488 awarded by Judge WILLIAM STABB to Miss PEARL KAVANAGH.

- The trouble is her ex-husband, Dan Maskell, 27, is out of work and does not have any money.

- The judge ruled he was to blame for an accident on the M23 in October 1975, when he drove his car into the back of an articulated lorry. His ex-wife was a passenger and suffered an ankle injury which has left her with a limp and disfiguring scars.

- As he was not insured or licensed to drive at the time, he claims his wife should not have got into the car. He had a record of accidents and said his wife should have known he was a bad driver. But the judge rejected his claim.

• It is hoped the motor Insurers Bureau will meet the bill, but the judge was told there was some doubt because of delay in claiming from them.

• "I hope they do," said Mr Maskell, of Bromley Road, Bromley, Kent, outside court. "Because if I have to pay she'll get the money at less than 10p a week."

• As a result of the accident the judge said Miss Kavanagh, of Lea High Road, Anerley, south-east London, has had to give up skating and tennis and also found dancing difficult.

• The cost of special sandals and shoes was £200 a pair and special boots cost £300. Her ex-husband should pay for the cost of a pair of sandals and shoes every year for the next 10 years and a pair of boot every other year.

12.02.81

Daily Telegraph

11.02.81

9.15 Cycled to bring Miss Burke's bag to 3 Chesterfield Street. Miss Burke did typing for me and had left her bag at the shop the day before. Maintained bike on return as it was not rolling well. Fitted A J Smith's shoes on him. Called to High Court in The Strand at 10.05. Cycled there and found Court 12. Case of MASKELL v MASKELL. Lady injured in car accident caused by negligent former husband. We had given an estimate to her in May 1980 and I was called as an expert witness to justify the price. Costs for attending will be refunded to the firm. Called in at MacIntyre Hudson the firms auditors, at 12.45 but they were at lunch. Called at 49 Tottenham Street our other branch to see what the staff there had done. That building had been used in the late eighteen hundreds as the German Working Mens Club. While Karl Marx lived in London writing "Das Kapital" he would have frequented the place. Rang Hentschy (my wife) to tell her about the case. Called into the Appliance Department at Middlesex Hospital. Collected shoes for Mrs Stubbs that needed adjustment.

Returned to 4 Paddington Street, 1.15, and had lunch on third floor.

Came down to a barrage of questions from Maggie, Mr Becker and Mr Carpenter who worked with me. Booked two orders for Mr Dent via Westminster Hospital and one order from Mrs Weinberg.

Spent rest of the afternoon 'phoning shoe repairers, giving them our name and address, so that enquirers for bespoke shoes can be directed to us.

Mr Tempest Radford collected his wife's boots. She has given other shoe makers, including Peter Shaw, problems. I hope all goes well with the boots and her.

I should be able to have a quiet evening at home. Maybe even with a fire. Hentschy had two Swiss ladies with their children in for coffee this afternoon. Monique Baumann and the Swiss lady (Sylvia Griffiths) from Rofant Road

12.02.81

Last night I discovered I had a Hernia. Just a dull ache, but quite a shock. There seems to be no reason for it. This morning I rang Dr Hatchick and then went and saw him. He confirms it was a Hernia and made an appointment for me to see a surgeon called Mr Slack. Now that is an appropriate name. He said I would need four or five days in hospital and a couple of weeks to recover. In the meantime, I could work normally, including riding a bike.

After lunch, I went to collect the passports from Petty France. I was in and out in five minutes. Then on to Westminster Hos. St Thomas's Hos. and on to Freeds in St Martin's Lane to collect ballet shoes for Maggie. I learnt Rodney Freed had set up a factory in Watford and the new owners of Freeds had forbidden Rodney to set foot in the Freed shop or factory.

Peen the last makers in Meard Street was my next call. Mr Bird, a pleasant young man heard about the episode with Mr Wavell and how I had given him his money back for the Lasts which we had incorrectly made. He had demanded the money back without coming and showing me the problem. I gave Mr Bird some cards and promised to send any people to him who just wanted Lasts.

The Middlesex Hospital Appliance Department was my last port of call, where I delivered new shoes for Rev Peter Rose of Cornwall. They will post them to him.

At 48 Tottenham Street, I switched on the window light. It may draw a few moths.

The shop was fairly quiet when I returned. Two enquiries as a result of leaving my name with repairers. By ringing them up, it seems to be fairly effective.

I'm now waiting for Hentschy in the shop. We are going on to see Hobson's Choice at The Lyric.

It was a very good performance. Some parts played better than at the performance we saw at The Vanburgh, e.g. Willy Mossop. The Lyric is an amazing theatre being an old tyme plaster and an ornate place in a new concrete building.

Afterwards, we found a pancake house and had a bite. We drove home and our son Michael welcomed us with "Good to see you."

13.02.81

Met Betty Sewell on the 8.12 fast Baker Street train. Discussed Northwood Council of Churches affairs. Very little post seems to come these days. Went up to the second floor to get a photocopy from our tenant who had a machine. The power point had obviously fused. Too many plugs on one adaptor. I checked the other plugs and found the same. I decided to fit double sockets.

During the morning, the most notable customer was Sheik Algosaibi, who came in for a fitting of his Lizard casuals ordered in November '79. Luckily, he has paid for them. He also bought two pairs of Green 's shoes, full brogue casuals, with shoe trees and had rubber heels put on them.

After lunch, I called into Ken McReddie to ask him about the plugs in his rooms on the third floor of the building. His sockets also are grossly overworked. He was anxious that the improvements would not put up his rent. He also suggested getting the doorbell to work and a set of keys for emergencies in case people were locked in i.e. In Emergencies, Break Glass.

I spent most of the lunch hour getting the doorbell to work. I had to find a key, then get a new battery, and then adjust the actual bell.

At 2, I left with Mrs Pelliser's boot and shoes for University College Hospital. On the way, I bought eight double sockets at an electrical wholesaler in Barratt Street. A useful place.

Mrs Pelliser was surprised to see me and showed me round Wallace Heaton where she worked. The video section was very interesting with the salesman there recommending SANYO CE10 at £625 as the best buy.

The chain came off the bike in Mortimer Street and I could repair it at 49 Tottenham Street.

Tomorrow, we go to Liverpool to visit my brother, Martin & family. He is doing a degree in Tropical medicine. Seems strange as he recently returned from Bangledesh after six years.

14.02.81 – 15.02.81

We had a good journey up the motorways 345 kms in 3½ hours each way with one stop. Martin's directions were good and we found 42 Egrement Promenade. A very large spacious Victorian flat with panoramic views over The Mersey. They were very pleased with the place, especially compared to others on the Tropical Medicine course who were paying as much rent for just one pokey room. They have two large bedrooms, a dining room, living room, kitchen and bathroom.

The area has seen better days when Wallasey was the fashionable district. Now, many houses and shops were boarded up, and gave a seedy impression. The same applied to what we saw in New Brighton and other parts we drove through. We took a very smooth road back to Wallasey and stopped at a level crossing that had to have the huge old gates opened for us by women who we summoned by ringing a bell.

16.02.81

Travelled up to London with Mr Siddiqui From Frithwood Avenue and Betty Sewell. Shop was pretty cool. Fair amount of post including cheques from Saudi Defence office for two pairs of shoes and Mr Peter Lewis, grandson of John Lewis. The electrician from the 2nd floor came and then told me that the wiring to the offices was on a single loop and would not take extra power points., They will need a ring main if we are to install the extra power points. I will get estimate from Usher Bros, Mr Emerick and Keith, the electrician from Brian Lack.

I spent some time upstairs 'phoning up about insulation and tongue and grooved boarding. To do the loft at home will cost about £300. I hope it is worth it.

Later, a husband and wife came in enquiring about shoes. They had been referred by their osteopath, Mr Savoury to Savva in Chiltern Street, who had sent him on to us. We could circularise all the Osteopaths and Chiropractors, or I could 'phone a few up each day.

Tonight is a Standing Committee meeting of the Northwood Council of Churches. I'm not too sure of what's on the agenda, which is not a very clever position for the Chairman. I think our secretary, Betty, will have more to say than I will.

17.02.81

It was a very pleasant and productive meeting. We will distribute, via newsagents if possible, Easter notices of services, aimed, if possible, at new estates.

Today was very busy in the shop with a good flow of cash and orders. Some upset too with Mrs Schreiber bringing her support back and asking for her money back. I refused on the grounds that all the alterations had given her her money's worth. We will see if we hear more. Also, Mr Cobell rang re Miss Reiss and I agreed to abandon the order and invoice. I will collect the shoes in due course. As Maggie was not in, it was all hands to deal with a steady flow of customers. We took in a lot of repairs (20 pairs) and a lot were collected. Also, our new push button 'phone was delivered. We ordered it 11.09.80, so that was five months.

I cycled over to C F Anderson at Islington Green and ordered and paid for tongue and grooved boarding and insulation material - £260 worth. I hope it does the job.

A man from The Legal & General Assurance Company came to inspect our security in response for a request for a quote for cover for theft. He may make some recommendations. The most obvious is a window lock on the ladies loo windows. I do not want an alarm system. Too much noise.

18.02.81

Mr Wilson was very happy this morning. He and his wife had won a trip to Los Angeles for two weeks at Top Rank Bingo. It was the first prize and he is going in April. I rang the Shoe & Leather News and told them. Mrs Jardin came in today and I could write my letter to the Planning Department about 1 Carew Road. During the morning, a shabbily dressed man with a deformed arm and left leg iron came in. He enquired and then ordered a pair of boots. A shoe repairer had given him our name. He paid for the drawing and will send a cheque for the balance.

At 2.30, I had an appointment at The Wellington Hospital to measure up Mr Kiryluk. A stroke caused him to need boots with a leg iron. I aim to finish these in two weeks.

The Moulinex blender I left on the train yesterday turned up at the Lost Property at Baker Street. What luck and honesty.

I rang up the Shoe & Leather News about Mr Wilson's good luck and told Bert Chapman about my chairmanship of the Northwood Council of Churches.

This evening, Hentschy and I go to Frithwood School to hear about learning thro' play.

It was a talk putting into very adult terms what children do when they play.

19.02.81

At 9.30, I went round to see Mr Slack at 18 Upper Wimpole Street. He examined me and confirmed my need for a Hernia operation. He will also do the ganglion on my right wrist as an encore. Mr Slack said he could only operate in central London and not out at Northwood, so I decided to opt for St John & Elizabeth, which he suggested. I had my tonsils out there when I was four. I quite liked it then, so I hope I'll enjoy it again.

The front wheel of the Moulton ruptured, so I had to walk back from the surgeons.

A reasonably harmonious day at the shop.

Miss Burke came in and typed the letters. Her knee seems to be getting better, but she is so frail.

20.02.81

On my journey into London I would read my way through the Bible. Finished reading the book of Daniel on the train. A busy start in the shop with three people in enquiring about repairs. Mr Gilbey brought in a cheque for his wife's shoes. It was two pounds too much, so I refunded him cash. Kenneth Goode came in today. He will prepare for the

Auditors. A busy morning. I took the wheel off the Moulton to take home. Mrs Haslam came in with her son and bought a pair of black Brogues. Tim is at Eton. Then Harry Brown needed his shoes softened on the stiffeners. Mrs Walters came in and ordered and paid for another pair of dark brown lizard sandals with pop buckles.

I had lunch upstairs with Kenneth and Gerald Joyce who was being shown how to do the book keeping. Kenneth is retiring owing to ill health. It was quite sociable.

After lunch, Mr Waller came in and I did several adjustments to get his boots comfortable.

As the Moulton is unusable, I took the orange collapsible bike. With the saddle raised, it went well. Having forgotten to take the padlock, I rushed into the London Foot Hospital and left an invoice and an envelope with a piece of leather. Then on to Tottenham Street where I parked the bike and went to the Surgical Appliance Office. It was quite a trek to find them in the basement of outpatients. I told them about my Hernia and helped them open a stuck drawer. I collected one boot for Mr Fort but left Miss Reiss's shoes for them to try to sell for me.

Now to take Hentschy and children to the airport. They will stay with Sanne, Hentschy's sister.

The family left and had a good flight on a Lufthansa Airbus to Hamburg.

I returned and made a start insulating and panelling Jenny's room. In two hours, all I achieved was three batons on the ceiling.

21.02.81

John Dean arrived on Friday night, wearing his RAF uniform. I made breakfast with sausages and bacon for the girls as well and then went into Watford to see Richard Neil. The front wheel of the Moulton bike is having new tyres put on and I ordered a brand new Raleigh fold-up bike. The first bike I personally had bought that was new. Richard will fit a dynamo lighting set and a moped saddle on as well and it will cost the firm just over £100.

22.02.81

The rest of Saturday and Sunday was spent insulating and panelling Jenny's room. The ceiling and back walls are finished. Now for the window wall.

23.02.81

I managed to catch the fast Baker Street train and had a good read in the Bible. A good post for cheques, including one from Miss Freud's solicitors on account for two pairs of shoes. There were relatively few people in the shop, maybe because of the cold.

I left the shop at 3 and went and paid Hentschy's parking ticket at 185 Marylebone Road. It was quite easy. Robert Lawrie was the next call for a couple of pairs of Vibram Soles. At British Home Stores, I brought a flight bag for Mr Wilson. It is his birthday on Wednesday and he may use it when he goes to the USA. I bought a china cup and saucer for Miss Burke's birthday on Thursday at John Lewis.

This afternoon, just before we shut, Mr Perry, a Palmay customer left shoes for Long soling. He lives in Paris and kindly paid with the repair. The discount helped.

Now for a solitary meal and on with the carpentry.

Martin 'phoned and I could tell him about his salary and my op. He said the parcel had arrived safely.

24.02.81

Caught the 8.12 early today. Several cheques in the post, including one from Peter Lewis, the grandson of the founder of John Lewis department stores. Mrs Garrett collected her shoes. She was pleased with them and bought some old cobbler polish for them. Mrs Forty also tried on her shoes, was happy and bought green polish for those. They need to be posted to St Thomas's. Mr A J Smith 'phoned to say University College Hospital were still not letting him have his shoes. I will have to call in. It is two weeks since I delivered them and Mrs Richardson and her assistant seem to be playing silly games.

Mr Joe Hyman called in with some golf-soled shoes to have the soles lowered. I wish he would get on and order a new pair. Then I can insist on my terms and make up for lost money on the last order when he said we had not made what he wanted, and left a pair on our hands.

A Mrs Apsley called in to collect two pairs of shoes she left for stitching soles a year ago. We could only find one pair. She was apologetic and we pointed out the Disposal of Uncollected Goods notice. She will ring in a few days to see if we find her brown court shoes.

During lunch, I read The Sunday Times supplement about Hiroshima and the Pope's visit. The hanger for the towel in the third floor fell off so I stuck it with neoprene.

Our fan for the shop ceiling was delivered and I rang Richard Usher, the electrician, to ask him to install it. I spent some of the afternoon ringing up shoe repairers asking them to recommend customers to us for made to measure.

Finally, Jerry Dudley rang to ask me to ring Alan Drew on Thursday to ask him to second me in the proposal at the British Surgical Technicians' Association AGM. That contractors supplying made to measure articles change regular contract prices to hospitals where fitting is to be done by hospital staff or self-employed orthotists.

This evening, I'm going to the Residents' Association AGM. I'm looking forward to the talk on the history of Northwood. It will make a break from panelling Jenny's room.

25.02.81

"How to Make an Effective Presentation" was the course I went to today. Held at the Charing Cross Hotel with only five students. The lecturer was a bouncy Welshman called John Williams. I sat next to Fred Eke, a former accountant at Huntsmans. How good the course was remains to be seen at my next presentation, but it was most enjoyable and satisfying in that I felt I learnt a lot.

On the course, there was Nick, an ex-actor, now working for Small Businesses Agency and a chap selling car components called Adrian from Pan Publishers.

In the evening, I went back to the shop to collect the boots for Mr Kiryluk.

At home, I then got on with the panelling of Jenny's room and finished the wall with the window. Hentschy 'phoned to say they were back in Hamburg, as Sanne her sister, had to see the doctor on Thursday.

26.02.81

I left home early to take the car into Moss Motors to be serviced. The courtesy bus ran me to the Met Station. The train I caught only ran as far as Wembley Park where we were told that because of signal trouble at Willesden Green, we should take the Jubilee. Met Peter Hall. I got off at St John 's Wood and walked to the Wellington Hospital. It was very cold. The boots went on with a struggle and he was pleased with them. It then turned out I needn't have struggled to get them ready so quickly as he will be in hospital quite a lot longer.

Richard Usher, the electrician, called at the shop and mounted the new fan with difficulty on the ceiling. It then turned out that a regulator was missing and the fan went much too fast and almost blew us away.

I went over to London Foot Hospital and then called at a fairly new shoemaker's called Savvas. He had worked at Deliss and had three other men working with him making fashion shoes. They looked very good.

Then on to Middlesex Appliance Office, down in the basement of Outpatients where I forgot to take the shoes made unsuccessfully for Miss Reiss.

27.02.81

It was a busy day in the shop, with Mrs Bryon in the morning bringing in her shoe for repair, and promising another order from the hospital. Mr Hirsch also came in and paid cash for his boots and a pair of plaited ready-made shoes. Both parties are hard work. The afternoon was also pretty good with three orders, all private in a row, including a Mr De Trafford who brought an embroidered slipper to be made up. We had 16 orders this week which is pretty reasonable.

This evening, Richard came over to the shop where we had a MacDonald's upstairs and then went on to The Bumble.

28.02.81

Nearly finished Jenny's room and cleaned up the house before Hentschy and the children returned. Jenny could even sleep in the room.

01.03.81

After breakfast, I showed Hentschy my new bike, a Raleigh foldaway. Went into London with the car in the evening to deliver the new bike. Judith babysat for us. Jenny was in the little back bedroom because I had started to sand the walls down. Hentschy and I collected shelving from Tottenham Street and brought it over to Paddington Street. Then we loaded on an old table, Martins Moulton bike, and the old carpet from the upstairs office. Quite a late finish.

02.03.81

The trains were up the spout this morning. A Diesel had caught fire between Moor Park and Rickmansworth and there were no fast trains and no trains north of Northwood. I was lucky and a train was turned round at Northwood to the dismay of the school children who wanted to go on to Moor Park and Ricky. It was packed and I saw Rodney Ward and John Winfield.

The shop was rather quiet with an order for Angela Imerie and Mrs A Ward from Sheffield.

Went over to Tottenham Street on the new bike. It ran very smoothly, the only problem was the stiff steering. I bought some edging strips at Weisberg Timber Merchant and brought them home on the train. I felt rather self-conscious carrying these long pieces and thought I might get turned out. Still it didn't happen and I got home safely with them.

03.03.81

Mr Ray Tite of the Footwear Training Board visited the firm and brought the modules for Induction, Pattern Cutting and Last Fitting. Through a great deal of repetition, he drilled into us how it was to be used. Mr Wilson was not very thrilled with the prospect and his main objection was "time". Later on, discussing it with Stephen, the trainee, I suggested three days a week, say Tuesday, Wednesday and Friday after tea in the morning until 1.30. That may give Mr Wilson a chance to do the most urgent work. After lunch, Ray showed Mr Becker how the manuals worked and found Mr B had too much to say.

Mr Kiryluk's boots were ready and I rapidly went up to the Wellington Hospital. |The right boot went on reasonably easily but the left one was impossible so a second zip will have to be fitted.

Hentschy had made pancakes as it was Shrove Tuesday. The children had also made some on their little stove. The first one we had, once the children were in bed, was savoury with egg, mushroom and prawns. Delicious. I then had seven with apple mousse.

Later on, having washed up, I re-hung the door in Jenny's room to the left so that it can open and I can panel over the hinge.

04.03.81

The train was slow again today because of trouble to another one ahead of us. Michael Green was waiting for me when I arrived at the shop and we talked for an hour. His main news was of a Riding Boot maker who could be packing up and would Taylors be interested in Bespoke making.

Mrs Jardin was in today and I dictated a couple of letters and tidied up the foot drawings and order forms. We had a very busy spell with Mrs Weinberg, Mrs Sass And Mrs Kopell, plus several new customers, all in at once. The post also brought a lot of cheques including one from the London Foot Hospital. I didn't go out in the afternoon and a certain Mrs Powell brought back a pair of sale shoes she had bought two years ago, claiming she had asked for all sorts of other things to be done. I had quite a barney with her and eventually she agreed to pay for having the stiffness cut down.

Mr Norton and Mr Peter Lewis also called in for fittings and were reasonably happy. Elaine Wratten was very delighted as well with her wedding shoes and the blue ones she collected. A lady called in with an outline of a foot and wanted a pair of shoes to fit for someone in Russia. We could not oblige, but she found on our trolley of bargains a pair that she liked and fitted for £5.

A photographer called in with a broken shoulder strap and wanted a new one made very quickly. After he had gone, I remembered a black strap down in the workroom, but it was too late, although Maggie ran out into the street to try to catch them.

Tonight, I hope to finish the woodwork in Jenny's room and start varnishing it.

05.03.81

A very quiet day in the shop. A Mrs Bryne from the Industrial Society came in at 10.30 and I discussed marketing with her. How to turn more telephone enquiries into orders. One idea was to get people saying yes, not telling them the price and persuading them to come in. She also suggested a survey of existing customers and finding out how long their shoes were lasting.

After lunch, I went over to the Wellington to deliver Mr Kiryluk's boot. We got it on this time and he was able to walk with reasonable security using the calliper and T-strap. He also gave me a glass of champagne, which was most acceptable.

The bike ran well and I then went back to the shop and on to Tottenham Street where I cleared up some more ready for our eventual leaving. I also found £4.57p in a trouser pocket. Whose was it? It paid for some wood I bought at Weisberg in Goodge Place.

Just before we closed the shop, Sir Anthony Lindon came in for seat pieces to cure a painful spur. Mr Sweetnam rang to say he would be coming. I have got Simon Brandenberg's shoes with me and they are to be collected this evening. I must also get from the garage some repairers Lasts which are wanted for a film set.

06.03.81

Kenneth Goode came in again today and worked out the 1980 balance sheet and a budget of how we had done. The budget was overall well balanced, and the balance sheet showed we had continued to make a profit. It was a quiet morning and Maggie went to the library to fetch a couple of books on Marketing.

After lunch, I cycled up to the Wellington Hospital because Mr Kiryluk's boot was still too difficult to put on. I had a coffee with him, although he reckoned that it was twenty cups of coffee a day that may well have contributed to giving him the stroke. I went back to the shop and then went on to the Westminster Hospital with a batch of invoices and a bag of scrap leather for the nursery class at the hospital. Miss Swanell said she would deliver it for me.

A Flat at 95 Eton Square was my next call at 3. I was about a minute late. The very spacious flat was the home of a Mrs Charles who had also had a stroke. A Chinese maid lived with her and her daughter was also there. She was anxious not to let the old lady know the price of the shoes and asked me to be discrete. After I had measured up and been ushered out of the front door by her, she gave me an envelope with £220 cash, for which I gave her a receipt.

I went back via Hyde Park and the crocuses were a picture. I popped down to John Lewis and bought the wrong nails, as it turned out, for Ben's birthday, and also a gallon of varnish for Jenny's room.

Hentschy arrived at 5.15 with the children who then amused the staff before they left. Michael knew all the names. We had supper upstairs and then drove via St John & Elizabeth Hospital, Grove End Road.

07.03.81

Went to Watford and collected the wheel for the Moulton from Richard Neale, bought a chiming doorbell in a shop opposite and then drove on to Moss Motors and ordered and paid for sun roof trims. When I got home, I fitted the wheels on to Moulton and hung it up in the garage. In the afternoon, while it poured with rain, Hentschy and I laid the carpet in Jenny's room and made it useable for her.

08.03.81

Sunday. I went to Quaker Meeting on my own. Hentschy drove me and I had a peaceful hour. I went home by train from North Harrow. In the afternoon, the weather was mild and we all went in the garden. I tried to strip paint from Jenny's skirting.

In the evening, I went round to see Amanda & Bruce and looked at an old trunk that needed leather pieces which I said I could get.

09.03.81

The post was good. Two orders from Mrs Hallynan in Northern Ireland with a cheque to cover them, a new order for Mrs Knapp from Oxford and another four orders during the day.

I left the shop at 10.30 and caught a taxi to Centre Point to go to the AGM of the British Surgical Trades Association. It was a packed meeting. The main news was the expected increase in next year's contract price at 17%. There was so many any other businesses that we broke for lunch and I brought my motion about No. 8 on the list. After I had said my piece and Peter Shaw had seconded me, those who spoke up were mainly against the motion. As a result, Jack van de Molen, the Chairman, suggested to me that I withdraw the motion to save the embarrassment of putting it to a vote. In some ways I regret not letting it go to a vote because it would have split the association between small contractors and large trade firms.

I felt pretty crushed and my eyes ached from the sawdust still in them. It was pouring down with rain and I left the meeting with Mr Moore from Salisbury. He still had not sold his business.

I went by bus to Bond Street and walked the rest of the way to the shop. There were a couple of new orders waiting and straight away, a string of people to see.

In the evening, Hentschy had invited the Bible Bashers, Kathy and Andrew, Lyn and Alister and Judith. We had a lovely supper of ham, pineapple, peas and potatoes, followed up with pineapple and strawberry mousse with quark. The offcuts from Jenny's room made a merry blaze and Alister was the liveliest of the evening with stories of Miss Almond. She is amazingly tactless, saying to newly engaged couples that they are ruining their lives, or they should get on with it in their rooms.

WITHDRAWN

09.03.81

That manufacturers charge hospitals the full contract price, when bespoke made to measure items are to be fitted by hospital staff as self-employed orthotics.

1. Safeguard all contractors – large and small.

2. Influence the DHSS to stop this practice before it spreads.

3. Encourage orthotists to remain with firms and not to go self-employed.

4. Help trade work prices to be increased? Colleagues. Do you want?

5. Ensure a larger number of BSTA firms remain viable?

6. Wider base of supply, therefore ensuring supply in times of shortages.

Sources of Orders:

1. Repeat Private

2. Repeat NHS

3. Hospital recommendation NHS

4. Hospital recommendation Private

5. Advertising

6. Personal recommendation

7. Doctors etc. recommendation

8. Shop window

9. Free publicity

1. How to increase repeat private

(a) Circular letters

(b) Circular phone calls

(c) Remind when calling for repairs

(d) Offer new materials or discounts

(e) Remind NHS customers to have additional specials

2. How to increase NHS repeat:

(a) Suggest when first order complete, a request for a second pair.

(b) Remind when brought in for repair.

(c) Ask appliance officers.

(d) (Circulars **not** allowed)

(e) Send lists of over five years to appliance officers to see if we can turn out.

10.03.81

I packed my briefcase this morning with my pyjamas and sponge bag ready for the hospital. I was late leaving and just caught a train. Bill Price was busy talking to another man about his plans for an extension over his garage.

The train was very slow and at Wembley Park, we were all turned off and packed on to the Jubilee Line due to signal trouble at Finchley Road. There seems to be more and more problems lately with the trains.

The post had several enquiry letters and as soon as Miss Burke arrived, I dictated them all to her. The shop was reasonably quiet and I slipped out on the bike. First to Blandford Street to deliver some old shoes to the sisters for their tramps, and then on to John Lewis, to return the rails which I had bought on Friday and to buy some maroon wool for Hentschy.

Gerald Joyce returned from his trip to Finchley where he had been for a rent tribunal to establish a new rent for his tenants.

The most alarming thing was, when I rang Mr Daly, who is supposed to be moving into the 1st floor offices after Jane Cormack leaves at the end of March. He said he had written to Disbrey to say that because the GPO might take a year to install the necessary lines, he could not move in. I went to see June and she said she only wanted to take the numbers, not the lines with her. I feel Mr Daly must have wanted to get up a lot more than an accounts department. We will try and find other tenants. Gerald Joyce, I hope, will sort it out.

I left the shop after one delay after another and caught a taxi up to the Wellington Hospital. Mr Kiryluk was able to get the boot and calliper on much easier. Really, I must remember next time to use double zips more often with stroke cases. It is much easier to put them on.

I arrived at the St John & St Elizabeth at just after 3 and reported at the enquiries where a porter took my rucksack up to Room 47 on St Andrew's floor. From the window, I can see over the rooftops to the Houses of Parliament. The faint noise of traffic can be heard. I was given a cup of tea and a piece of chocolate cake by a nurse called Elenore who then took down loads of particulars. Then a Doctor van der Slay gave me a good grilling of questions, examined me and confirmed my Hernia.

I made good use of the 'phone to Hentschy, Jane Cormack and the shop. I had some eye drops which have soothed them quite a bit, but I can still feel the bits of grit in them.

Supper was good and filling. Onion soup and toast, chicken and chips, peas, carrots and then jelly and cream, washed down with coffee. A sister came in and had a look at my ganglion. I wonder how much that will slow my writing down.

I'm now looking forward to seeing Hentschy. I banished the telly. I can live with it, even though there is news of the Budget. This writing is good for my soul.

11.03.81

The day of the op. Mr Slack looked in and marked where I was to be cut. He decided to leave the ganglion because I had managed to knock it down a week ago. The Anaesthetist came and looked me over. Dr Cope was his name and nature. My op was scheduled for 11.15, so my pre-medical was set for 10.15. Before that, a young porter came to shave my tummy. Then I had a bath and asked the nurse if he had shaved me enough. With a few minutes to go, another porter came and gave me a more thorough shave.

The pre-medical consisted of three jabs in my bottom and then the curtains were drawn and I dozed for nearly an hour. The nurses came back with a porter and I was taken down in the lift to the theatre. With no more ado, I was given a jab and I said, "I can feel myself going."

The next thing I knew was I was back in my room and it was 3 o'clock. I had a bandage over my tummy with a pad to the left. I was very dozy the rest of the day and when Hentschy came to visit me, I asked her to read so I could keep my eyes closed.

Before she left, she had a little cry. She had brought lovely daffodils with a sprig of a bush.

The Night Sister came later and gave me a wash and then a jab against pain and a sleeping pill. I slept really well and at 6 o'clock, she brought me a cup of tea.

12.03.81

I felt most refreshed and had a breakfast of four pieces of toast with a cup of tea. The nurses were very busy with buzzers going off all the time. They wanted to make my bed and I stood up for the first time. I had just shuffled to the window when they were called away again. After nearly ten minutes, I began to feel faint, so I went back to bed.

For lunch, I had boiled fish, potato and peas. A few peas fell on the floor.

I tried to ring Mr Kiryluk at the Wellington Hospital, but had to speak to the Sister on his floor. All is well with his boots.

Mr Wilson called in and brought a huge bunch of flowers which the nurses then put into to vases.

When Mr Wilson had exchanged all his conversation, in came Joe Sewell. Joe left about 4, by which time I was desperate to spend a penny. I could not seem to do it into the bottle lying down. Good training not to wet beds? I sweated hot and cold and even misfired into my pyjamas. Nurse Moore came and helped me get up and then I could perform very happily and nearly filled up the 20 oz bottle. I felt greatly relieved.

Gerald Joyce arrived to visit and the supper came up. I found it hard work to eat because of wind. In fact, I almost asked Gerald to leave. I then got up on my own and spent another good penny and felt much better.

Hentschy arrived and we had a reasonable happy chat and I showed her how I could get up and spend a penny. What an honour.

There is a change of staff and the new Night Sister has brought me a drinking chocolate. I expect I will sleep well tonight.

13.03.81

I did sleep well and today seemed to be one of feeding me up. Breakfast: Grapefruit, cornflakes and All bran and toast and tea. I was getting up every couple of hours for ten minutes or so to have a walk to the loo. I also explored the old Children's Ward 8, also on this floor, but closed down and derelict. I quite fancy an old clock in there.

Lunch was very good. Grilled Trout with chips and a side salad, followed by lemon meringue pie. It was delicious.

Dr Hatchick called in. He was most charming and told me that Mr Slack was a near neighbour of his. I also gave him his new shoes and I hope he has no problem with them.

Kathy and Andrew also came. I nearly laughed too much at their chatter. During their visit, Dr van der Slay came and had a look at me. All being well, I should be able to leave on Sunday.

I went down in the lift with Katy & Andrew and we visited the Chapel. It is amazingly large and there were some holy relics.

I 'phoned up the shop and thanked them for the cards and flowers. I also had a 'phone call from Mr Ibrahim.

I could not eat up all my supper of fricassee chicken, rice, and tomatoes but I did polish off the fruit salad. I had a sleep before my lovely Hentschy came. She brought more cards and flowers.

Now for another night's sleep. I hope I can go to the loo tomorrow.

14.03.81

I slept pretty well without a sleeping pill. I got up before breakfast and went to the loo with the wooden seat. On the way back, I passed the kitchen and checked if they had given me bran. As they had not, I could take the packet to my room and then return it. Another step to independence. After the bran and the breakfast, I was able to open my bowels, as they put it, for the first time. I felt much happier. Then I asked Sister if I could have a word with her. She came to my room, then about 9.30 and I asked her if I could buy, for £50, the clock in the abandoned Children's Ward. She was pleased with the idea and said she would ask Matron. I rang up Hentschy and told her it would be alright to bring the children in the afternoon.

I had a walk over to the old Children's Ward again. Had a rest, then after an hour or so, walked downstairs one floor and looked at the older wards. It is a magnificent bit of Victorian/Edwardian grandeur with plenty of religious accessories. St Theresa's Ward was the best. Across a wood-panelled bridge, it led to a nurse's office and then an internal balcony with a stained glass roof. The rooms ran down small corridors leading off the corners of the square balcony. An alter with the sort of lovely clock I have my eye on was ticking beautifully. I got back to bed nearly 20 minutes after leaving it, feeling pretty worn out.

Lunch consisted of oxtail soup and toast. Roast Beef, rice and boiled potatoes. I had forgotten to ask for greens. That was followed by bread and butter pudding and a cup of tea.

The nurses, Elenor and Linda, were on duty. Elenor was sure I would not be leaving before next week. I assured her I would be out the next day.

I rested well before the family were due at 3. The children came in very quietly and were extremely good and kind. Michael had a surprise when he pressed the buzzer to call the nurse. He couldn't turn the light out by repeated presses and burst into tears. Elenor rushed in thinking I had had a fit to find Michael crying on his Mummy's lap.

Hentschy and I had a coffee and the children had orange juice and biscuits. We had a little walk together up to the loo and on the way back, met Dr Cope who was looking for me. Michael was full of questions. Why are you a Doctor? What did you do to my Daddy? etc. etc.

He confirmed that I could go home on Sunday.

After Hentschy left with the children, I listened to the radio, had an omelette for supper and listened to Stop the Week and laughed quite a bit at their stories.

Hentschy came again. Amanda babysat for us as the Bible Bashers were at a service. It was good to talk quietly with Hentschy and to get up and put pants on. They seem to support me and then the op doesn't pull so much.

I listened to Saturday Night Theatre. A good old "who dunnit" and then slept well.

15.03.81

Just before breakfast, I went for a walk up the corridor to stretch my legs. At Room 50, a man I had nodded to before was happy to chat. It soon turned out that he was Mr Lees from Nottingham for whom the firm has made shoes for years. He is having treatment for his Rheumatoid Arthritis and hopes to leave next week.

As soon as I had eaten my large portion of All bran and cornflakes, I had to go to the loo and succeeded again in doing a big one. Feeling greatly relieved, I then knocked back my egg and bacon, toast and two cups of tea.

The nurses came and made my bed and then Sister came and took the dressing off the wound. The scar is very neat and has healed well. She used ether to wash the sticky off. It certainly ponged. Three other people, including a consultant, are after the clock, so I could not have it, but I will still leave a cheque for £50 towards their good work. The best news though was that I can leave this morning, so I have rung up Hentschy and she would be on her way soon.

The journey home was OK in the orange Beetle, especially when I just relaxed and didn't press on the floor with my legs. When we got home, I went straight in the front room and lay on the pollsters, which is where I have spent most of my days.

I have got out of the daily habit of keeping my diary.

Most of the time I have taken it very carefully because my tummy hurts. Yesterday morning (Thursday, 19.03.81) two fire engines went up Carew Road. We wondered if they had gone to Michael's school. Hentschy didn't get as far as the school before she was turned back. The library was on fire. An electrical fault we were told had smouldered and caused a lot of smell and mess. Michael is home today as well.

20.03.81

The pain is not so intense and I had twenty minutes in the garden with Jenny whilst Hentschy and Michael went shopping in Pinner.

21.03.81

Saturday. I did not feel so good but in the afternoon I pushed myself into the garden to fill up some seed boxes. I stayed out for 40 minutes. Hentschy planted 50 bulbs in the flower bed, Gladioli etc.

In the late afternoon, Gerald & Hazel came over and brought various papers and had some tea with us.

I noticed, after they left, that my scar was getting red and swollen and quite painful.

22.03.81

I thought I must have overdone it and got myself a second rupture and/or an infection in the wound. In the afternoon, we tried to ring Dr Hatchick, but there was no answer. When I went to bed, Hentschy made me a camomile tea which we used as a poultice with a hanky. It soothed me quite a bit.

23.03.81

My scar was really shining, bulging and very red. I could not sit comfortably and quickly went back to bed after breakfast.

After several attempts, I got through to Doctor Hatchick, who told me my inflammation was common and it would pass after a few days. During the day, it just got more painful. The weather became very stormy with soot falling down the chimney in the front room where I was lying. Then, in the evening, we began to get a series of wrong telephone calls. Water on the wires. Hentschy had put the children to bed and went to wash her hair. I had another camomile poultice to sooth my tummy. The 'phone rang again. A gentleman's voice said, "Is that my home?" I answered, "No, it's mine."

I lay down and then hopped up to turn the telly off. I felt the poultice slip and saw that a load of puss had shot from my wound. I was quite alarmed and lay down very quietly. I dabbed off a stream of pink fluid that rose from the scar. I called Hentschy and she went to the car and brought the First Aid Kit. We put a clean gauze dressing on. Then we tried to ring Dr Hatchick at his home, repeated no answers. Then we rang Dr Goodwin. The receptionist at 8.30 in the evening asked if I could come down to the surgery. Hentschy explained I could hardly stand and certainly not sit. Hentschy didn't get any advice but a promise that the doctor would call in the morning. We were still very worried. Would the scar open up? Would all my guts fall out if I stood up? Hentschy then tried Dr Hatchick and got through. He was rather abrupt until Hentschy announced who she was. He said the eruption was good and we should not worry.

I went to the loo and with sitting, the floor turned dark crimson. I went steadily upstairs to bed and put a large pad on and moved as little as possible, not even brushing my teeth. The pad was full by the morning.

24.03.81

I had breakfast in bed. The flow was still very yellow, but the pressure was gone and late in the morning, I got up and dressed. I just got down when Dr Goodwin arrived. He had had the letter from Dr Hatchick and prescribed some antibiotics to knock out the infection. He also advised a daily bath.

01.04.81

I have been getting better, steadily better. Last week I took Jenny to London to the shop and also went to Toddlers Club with her.

Yesterday, 31.03.81, I went with Jenny to 4 Paddington Street to see the new prospective tenant for the 1st Floor. A Miss Irene Clunie. She looked quite interesting with a brown corduroy hat on top of long blonde hair. I took her upstairs, and with Jenny on my lap, she told me about her business as an employment agency for hiring drivers and bodyguards.

02.04.81

Jenny's birthday. Collected Michael from school and strained myself lifting the back gate. Slowed me down at her party because of the ache.

03.04.81

Went up to the shop with Jenny in the morning. Saw Dr Hatchick and was signed off. Spent some time sanding down the skirting board and doorframe for our room. In the evening, Lyn Hellmouth, our bible student, babysat when we went to the Frithwood School Social. Mr Long showed his violent and horrific children's films and one for Mrs Davis's wedding.

04.04.81

Mrs Lasman's 'phone was still out of order. I rang the exchange to see if it could be mended. Serviced the lawnmowers including the one I bought from Mrs Lasman for £25.

05.04.81

Went to meeting with the children and stayed in the children's class because they were so naughty. Michael is in a bad stage. In the afternoon, Age Link came to tea with 11 old folk and 9 helpers. It was a happy time with singing. The helpers also moved a fridge for us from the coal hole into the hall so Martin can have it.

06.04.81

Went to work. Met Betty Sewell and her daughter, Mary, and talked about the Northwood Council of Churches.

We took a few orders this morning and in my absence it turned out the most problems had been between staff. I will have to build a Corps de Spirit.

We took four orders today which was much better than previously.

Lynn came to babysit for us in the evening while we went to see Michael's teacher, Mrs Torrins. We were expecting an unpleasant interview. However, Mrs Torrins seemed to go all out to be as pleasant as possible and said Michael was settling in quite well and wanting to work. However, she reckoned that he was about two years behind in his development and behaviour. Maybe because he copies his three year old sister.

When we came home, we rang up a number in Focus concerning two brown sheepskin rugs for sale in Rickmansworth. We found 113 Tudor Way easily and then popped in on Paul Williams who was on his own babysitting. Lucy was at a school choir. He is now working for a firm called Stan Taylor insuring footballers against injury. His life seems very full with Church and School. He also showed us his Austin 10 which he is doing up. We looked at the beautifully cleaned and painted chassis. The body is in store at his mother-in-laws.

As we drove into Carew Road, we saw Kathy and Andrew coming back. Kathy will stay with us and share with Lynn.

07.04.81

Feeling much better down below and I just wish I could get rid of my sore throat. Travelled up to town on the slow No. 31 Baker Street with Ron Simpson. Saw Mary Sewell waiting at North Harrow.

Not much post, but Dr Seers came in and confirmed his order for another pair of cloth top boots. There were four other orders and it's looking better. In the afternoon, I worked most of the time upstairs on the new NHS schedules. It is quite tricky. Mr Stevenson called in to collect his shoes, which had sponge spur socks put in.

Mrs Charles also called in and we had her fitting.

Started clearing out the old desk in the evening.

08.04.81

A quiet day in the shop. Went round to Mr Maguire to collect his shoes which are giving problems. Asked Mr Carpenter to re-shape the Lasts and Mr Kochan will remake them. I used the bike for the first time and went over to

Tottenham Street via the London Foot Hospital and also called in at the Appliance Office, temporarily in the basement of Outpatients. At Tottenham Street, the drain was overflowing and I rang Gerard Disbrey for advice, who was responsible? and how to get attended to promptly.

09.04.81

Met a new fellow commuter who looked like Titus. We got chatting. His name is John Glass, a geologist for Gulf Oil, living in Roy Road with his wife, 6-year old daughter and 3-year old son. The girl goes to Frithwood School.

The shop was quiet first thing so I started going through the Training Manuals with Stephen Hedley. He was not very responsive and obviously bored. We worked through the first two sections up to teatime.

I rang Peter Logan and asked about Martin and his tax affairs. Then I rang Kay Shelley at the Ruislip-Northwood Gazette and told her reporter, Anne Powell, about my election as Chairman of the Northwood Council of Churches and its 30-year anniversary. She also asked about my background and experiences as a Chairman in other fields.

Gerald Joyce arrived back at the shop at about 11, having been to see his wife Hazel sworn in at the Middlesex Guildhall as a JP.

A Miss Alison Rutherford from Newcastle called by appointment at 1 o'clock and stayed most of the afternoon, gleaning information about the firm, its history, method and staff. It was all to do with methods of measuring for Rheumatism. She was very interested in the Birkemann

Tritspoor. A device that used ink on a sheet of rubber and showed foot pressure points.

During the evening I had a 'phone call from my Australian cousin Lee Golding who had arrived in London for a six-week holiday. I fixed up to meet her for lunch the next day.

10.04.81

Travelled up reading the book on letter writing. Betty Sewell and co were in the next compartment. The weather has turned warm and sunny. The shop was not very positive with Mrs Bryon and Mrs Bechel complaining about their shoes.

I managed to leave the shop at quarter to twelve and find the Plaza Hotel by twelve over near Queensway. Lee arrived a few minutes later. I recognised her easily enough. We went and had a pub lunch in the Albert in Queensway. Steak & Kidney, 2 veg. I found it a little bit hard work because she was not all that forthcoming or else she was a bit shy. I've invited her and said Martin will ring on Thursday evening. Lee was going on to her aunt Olive in Dover, catching a train at 2 from Charing Cross.

During the afternoon, a Mr Bisco called at the shop and asked to buy the name, James Taylor & Son. That I declined, but I had an idea he might buy Kember's as he had bought the premises at 4 Montpelier Street, Knightsbridge, where they had formally operated.

I also talked to Ken McReddie who said he was considering moving out, to Regent Street. He is quite astute and I will have to watch it.

I met Marian Hofer as I got off the train at Northwood. Quite a while since I've seen her, and she was interested in Martin's move to Keighley.

11.04.81

I had a restless night, maybe because of meeting Lee Golding. At 7.22 I shot out of my sleep, hearing a big lorry coming into Carew Road. The previous Thursday evening, a load of clay had been fly tipped at No. 1, Carew Road. I had rung the local police station and reported it.

On Friday evening, I had gone and had a look at No. 1 and a barricade of milk crates and bits of wood had been put over the entrances.

The heavy noisy lorry that had woken me, had two men in the cab, which was red, and I concentrated on getting the number, LHK 110P. Hopping out of bed to the landing, I then say it had gone into No. 1 and was tipping its load. I rang 999 and was passed to the local police station to whom I reported. As I spoke, the lorry came back and I could tell them it was going down towards Northwood Station.

It was quite drizzly and damp, so most of the morning we cleared out the museum in the dining room for Martin to take. After a very loud lunch, we went into the garden. Hentschy tucked the weeds under the loganberries and blackberries and then dug over the rest of the bed and removed the brick paths. Michael and Jenny carried the bricks round to the new shed where I will make a hard pavement.

I cut the lawn with our old Jetstream. It was quite hard to start. Either the timing or the plug is not right.

This evening, Hentschy packed a load of the Rosenthal China for Martin and I packed more photos. 10 o'clock bed.

12.04.81

Sanded down the old tray in the morning and showed Len Rosso and Carisbrook and where the proposed old people's home would be and the Driver development.

In the afternoon, we drove into London to bring some branches to decorate the shop, and to collect the angle poise lamp for Martin. We all went over to Regents Park and looked at the lovely flowers. Tulips, daffodils and flowering trees. In the evening, Martin rang to ask which high chair to buy for us. We sorted out the china cupboard and I carried on with the desk photos.

13.04.81

I caught the 8.12 fast Baker Street and met Betty Sewell. H G Jones was our earliest customer and collected one pair of new shoes.

I rang Gerard Disbrey, our solicitor, about a letter he had sent me concerning Miss Clunie, new prospective tenant for the 1st Floor. She had said I would pay legal costs. I denied that the subject had ever been mentioned. I also talked over with Gerard, the offer for Kember's Name. I sent him the agreement I had found, dated 1972.

After lunch, I went to see Miss Allen at St Pancras Hospital. She ordered another pair of shoes. I had expected her to ask for the other shoes we had made to be adjusted to make them higher.

I then cycled on up Pentonville Road and down City Road to Companies House to see if Kembers were still listed as traders.

The only entry I could find was marked Ceased in 1940. I went via Chiswell Street back to the shop doing 10 miles in all.

The Underground had a fault during the afternoon, but current and trains were running again to take me home.

This evening, we are expecting our Austrian visitors. A mother and her two sons. They arrived and seem very pleasant. Volker 16 and Mrs Pichel from Vienna. They will stay until Sunday. The boys are in Michael's room and Michael is in the playroom. Mrs is in the small bedroom.

14.04.81

Travelled up to London with John Glass and Betty Sewell. Quite a few cheques and a couple of hospital orders in the post. When I wanted to go to lunch, several customers came in who wanted to speak to me at once. Gordon Graham, Miss Galtrey and Mrs Koscer.

After lunch, I went over to LFH and delivered an adaption, then on to UCH where I just caught Mrs Richardson as she was leaving her office. She asked me to cancel the invoice and her offer for Mr Smith's shoes, as they were lost, and she would "see our firm all right."

I then went on to see Miss Wheeler at the Appliance Office at the Middlesex Hospital.

Ken McReddie is the problem at the moment. He wants to leave and give the minimum notice. I wold like a length of time to find a new tenant and he should leave the rooms in a reasonably decorated condition.

I must ring up Chris about lending his scaffold tower to John Glass this evening.

We watch "Caught on a Train," a film on BBC1. It was very good.

15.04.81

Our Austrian family were very punctual for breakfast and I gave the minutes of the Northwood Council of Churches to Kathy to deliver to her principle at the Bible College, with an invitation written on them to join us at the next meeting. I met John Glass on the train and told him he would have to hire the scaffold tower from the shop in the High Street. It has been a lovely sunny day. I did a bit more on the schedules before ten. I also had to go over to Robert Lawrie At Seymour Street to buy Vibram soles for climbing boots. On the way, I called at the Post Office opposite and sent off my saving books to have the interest calculated.

Mrs Jardin came in and sorted out old letters, keeping the most interesting for the historic letters file. I cycled over to Swinards to pay for tickets to Hamburg for Hentschy and the children, also I booked for our trip to Guernsey in July. John Lewis was my next stop for light bulbs and egg soap for all the various children who are coming over Easter.

I rang Mr Lobb about making shoes for Prince Charles through the West End Master Bootmakers. He was not too pushing and asked me to sound out the other members.

16.04.81

I caught the later fast Aldgate train and did a bit of reading about telephone sales. Maybe we will circularise most customers by 'phone.

It was a busy morning with a lot of customers in because we had said we were closing at 2. Mrs Bryon was in needing more adjustments to her shoes. Mrs V Young was in from Bury St Edmunds with repairs and so it went on. Mrs D Smith had an order for two pairs from St Thomas's, one to be fur-lined boots. The sun shone and we had only pleasant customers.

This afternoon, my brother Martin is due to arrive with a lorry to collect all the furniture and belongings for his new house.

Martin arrived at 4 o'clock with his 3-ton lorry. It took a lot of shunts to back in. Graham arrived at 5 and John at 6. All the heavy furniture was on at 7 and all was loaded by 9.30. Graham stayed the night.

17.04.81

Good Friday. Martin left at 6 and knocked the gate post down. The Austrian visitors went up to London. We had hot cross buns. It was very cold but sunny.

18.04.81

Saturday. After breakfast, we went to Pinner to shop at Bishops and also to look at vacuum cleaners. In the afternoon, it was warm and I cut the grass with the lawn mower I bought from Mrs Lasman.

19.04.81

Easter Sunday. We had a great invasion. Frank and his family for lunch. Auntie Lottie and Hans and Sue. Clive and tribe came for tea. It was a good binge with Sue holding forth on her job. Really, it was too many with not much time for Hentschy or I to talk to everyone. We were pretty tired by the time they all left.

20.04.81

I sanded down Jenny's skirting board and the old loo sent from 49 Tottenham Street in the morning. Karl Marx may have sat on it and thought about what he was writing in his book. There were quite a few heavy showers and I sat under the eaves of the shed.

Michael helped me with varnishing in the afternoon and knocked some over my new shirt.

Whilst on the roof, repairing a broken tile, I saw John Herrning at No. 14 Eastbury Road and went round with some glass and a tile to match the replacements he needed.

He kindly showed me over the house and I was amazed at just how big it is.

21.04.81

Back to work. Pretty cold in the shop. We took three orders. I stayed in in the afternoon and finished off the NHS contract.

Kenneth Goode came in and prepared a trial balance for the Auditors and a budget. It makes pretty alarming reading and challenges me to boost the sales. I must ring Mr Fustock and see if Prince Abdulla is coming, or if he would like his shoes made by us. Also, Dr Platts at the RNOH Stanmore must be another target. We had some free publicity in Vogue which resulted in an order this morning.

Maybe Maggie can win some orders by 'phoning people up. "Fight recession with aggression," as one advert put it.

23.04.81

Not a busy day again. Several enquiries and we are trying to win them with all our services. Mr Carpenter went to London Foot Hospital and brought back one order. I went over to UCH and delivered the repairs for Mr Harrington. Mrs Richardson is always on about politics, Social Democrats and the Common Market.

I went on to Great Russell Street to a coin merchant and bought an LSD set for Peter Hentschel.

49 Tottenham Street was my next call and I saw that the drain was still blocked and overflowing. Mrs Pelegrini begged me to get it seen to. I collected a batch of orders from Miss Wheeler at the Middlesex Hospital including a new order for Mr Concannon.

At John Lewis, I found the material Hentschy wanted and ordered an angle poise lamp for the office. Then on to Swinards Travel to collect the tickets for Hentschy.

24.04.81

A cold day. Five orders, two private. Mr Briem, from Iceland and Mrs Hallagan, Northern Ireland.

Went over to Tottenham Street in the afternoon to see the Dyno Rod man to let him in to clear the blocked drain. He did not succeed and a more powerful machine will come on Monday. Miss Pellegrini was not happy.

Called in at Allens and collected the Lasts and trees for Dr Seear. Mrs Herzberg was disappointed when I rang to say her boots were not ready because they were overlooked after she rushed in and out, because of her friend being illegally parked.

We were invited out for supper with Amanda and Bruce Hibbert and when we arrived, we found another guest, an elderly lady neighbour who lived at 6 Hallowell Road. David Dewey and his wife also came. I had met David, who I called Richard, at quite a few protest meetings in the past. We were well wined and dined. Smoked mackerel pate with white wine. Then stew, cabbage and potatoes with red wine. I had never seen the Hibberts' dining room before.

A large picture of Gladstone hung over the end of the room. A large oval birds' eye walnut dining room table, old chairs with grubby seats, a lovely cabinet with glass doors containing models of steam locomotives. Next to the window were pictures of old battleships. Bruce's naval interest. We had a very tasty chocolate pudding and then raspberry mousse to follow. The conversation ranged over a wide range of topics. Hentschy could chip in when it came to the Common Market.

Before we knew it, one o'clock was upon us and I felt we had to leave.

25.04.81

Hentschy and the children went to Hamburg and we had an early breakfast for a Saturday. I drove them down to Heathrow Airport in plenty of time in case of delays caused by the customs and immigration staff. I got home about 10.30 and packed and left by 11. I got a train straight away and arrived at Kings Cross at 12. Lee saw me first and we got on the train in plenty of time. She had a rail pass and could go First Class. I decided to go First Class too and it was very comfortable and could pay the difference of £3 which I thought was pretty reasonable.

We got to Keighley a few minutes late, but Martin was there to meet us. He looked a lot less tired than when we saw him on the Thursday before Good Friday. Lee had plenty of snow to look at, snow at the end of April, and at least a foot of it in Keighley. The car had a struggle to get up the hill to his new house. The house was in a new estate and was faced with local stone. Quite attractive. As with the flat in Wallasey, the greatest asset was the view, over the Aire

Valley with Keighley to the right and another small town to the left. Immediately below were fields. The four bedroomed house was spacious but cold. The wind howled around and through all the gaps in the doors and windows. The central heating was no match for the arctic blast.

We went for a walk as the sun was shining and walked up the hill and on to the Skelton road. A snow plough had cleared it but it was still only passable to land rovers and motor bikes. We saw lots of sheep and lambs.

After supper, Carolyn went to bed and we watched the lights in the valley. It was like flying. I talked through the plans for the next day with Martin and slept well.

26.04.81

After a good breakfast, in a dining room containing a lot of the furniture from Golders Green, we drove over to Bolton Abbey. The wind was bitterly cold. I had been there before on a geography field trip in 1962. It was a lovely setting and Lee saw quite a few geological things e.g. the River Cliff with coal seams and later on a fold of rock in an old quarry. She had studied geology at Melbourne University and had a PhD.

Liz made a great stew of chicken, potato and carrots and I felt quite bloated after lunch. After a mammoth washing up, which included a lot of Mum's old cooking equipment, we repaired a switch in the garage. Then we fixed some wall lights in the sitting room.

After what I felt was a rushed tea, Martin drove me to the station. Keighley is the junction for the Worth Valley. The station is well painted because of the private steam line that runs up to Howarth. The train got to Leeds in plenty of time for me to catch the 125 to London. All the snow is disappearing as we go south, and the train is getting full.

At Kings Cross, the train was 15 minutes late arriving. At the barrier, quite a few people went round the side of the ticket collector and so did I. From Keighley to London without one ticket check.

At the Met ticket office, I heard a train coming in, broke out of the queue and ran through the barrier, showing my season. As I was about to jump in, I checked my trouser pocket for my wallet, turned round and rushed back to the barrier, only to find it in my coat pocket. By the time I was back in the platform, the train was gone.

At Baker Street, I just had a minute to catch the Watford train. Just before Wembley Park, four skinheads came through from the next carriage. They held the door against a fifth who spat at the glass. At Wembley Park, the train stopped for a while and two policemen appeared. They asked the boys ages, and if they had tickets. As they had none, they ordered then off to buy some.

When I got home at 11, I found a bucket on the landing, and two up the stairs to collect water from the leaky roof.

27.04.81

Kathy and Lyn were in for breakfast, but I missed the usual fast Barker Street at 8.12. The post was quite heavy with several cheques for small amounts. Dyno Rod 'phoned to say their van was on site, and I to Tottenham Street to see it. Pipes over the pavement and in the basement. However, it cleared the block and the smell went later.

I popped into see Miss Wheeler and delivered Miss Reisse's shoes. When I got back to the shop, Peter Sprat, the Audit Clerk from MacIntyre Hudson arrived. Gerald Joyce and I had lunch with him. He is rather shy and lives in Hayes End.

In the afternoon, I went over to Mortimer Street to see about our ad in Rehab Magazine.

The time clock on the gas stove did its job and I did supper. Then I rang Martin and thanked him for the weekend. I also rang Ron Turner and offered him a lift to the Northwood Council of Churches meeting. When I started the car, I got showered by the sun roof.

The actual meeting was quite lively with more contributions than at previous meetings, and ideas flowed almost too freely.

28.04.81

Caught the fast Baker Street and met Betty Sewell. I left the shop at 10 after I had dictated my three letters to Miss Burke. First, I cycled to see Miss Swannell at Westminster Hospital and delivered Mr Keisner's boots. Their papers to give the order had been discovered and I collected one boot for Mr Toledarno.

The Royal Forestry Society meeting was timed to start at 11 at St James Park and I met up on time. We were guided round by a Mr Mitchell who was full of tales of woe on how various secretaries had all the say on how the park should be run. We saw some very dodgy looking willows at the

Buckingham palace end, leaning at an incredible angle, but no decisions being taken.

We could hear the band of the Coldstream Guards and see the Changing of the Guard at Horseguards.

The island where the ducks are reared was also shown to us. Broody hens on ducks eggs. Large empty pens and a warm shed were seen. Some lovely Rhododendrons but also a lot of mess.

After the tour of St James, we all got into cars. Paul Ackers put my bike in his car and we all went for lunch at The Crown in Hamilton Road, NW8. Hamilton Terrace with an Avenue of Planted 1877 London Planes was an impressive start for Paul's tour. Planes crown pruned before complaints received from residents. Acacia Road was full of exotics in private gardens.

Jubilee Cherry trees in Abbey looked in good form. Then he showed an estate called Mozart Place. Landscaping with too many trees, too close to buildings.

Paul dropped me at St Mary's Hospital, Praed Street and I saw Miss Hiscock who confirmed we could make for Mrs Givons. I also saw the Queen Mother as she passed between the two blocks of the hospital.

Back at the shop, they seemed to have had a busy day and I could clear up some of my desk.

At home, I varnished the cutlery again and made a few 'phone calls, including to Hentschy. Also, sorted out Christian Aid for Thursday, 14th May.

29.04.81

Caught the 8.18 fast Baker Street. Several orders to book, two for Mrs Charles, Mrs Parkman etc. Quiet morning until I said a few times "Come on customers, where are you?" Then they came in. An Arab from the Saudi National Guard

Had lunch with the Auditor, who seems to be getting on well with the work.

After lunch, I went on to the London Foot Hospital where I found the shoes I wanted to deliver had no invoice, so I took them on with me to the meeting at Centre Point of the British Surgical Trades Association. The meeting was full. Contractors seeking advice on how to price the new period. Met Peter Shaw and Roger Manning. Plenty of good discussion about inflation.

Left at 4.15 and went on to RADAR to discuss the copy with the copy writer.

I hope it brings plenty of orders. Then on to 49 Tottenham Street and then Miss Wheeler the Appliance officer at the Middlesex Hospital and back to the shop.

Mr Carpenter bought a rectangular piece of lambswool for £1 from the firm. It will make good rags or car seats.

Peter Henschel's birthday today, so I will ring him in Wahlstadt when I get in.

The hall floor had a good thick coat of varnish and looks good.

30.04.81

I drove the car over to Moss Motors in Watford and arrived at 8.15, just in time to catch the courtesy bus. The old Beetle was to have a rear lock on the engine compartment, rear seat belts, and the roof light trim replaced.

The bus took me to the Met station and I caught a slow Baker Street train, changed at Moor Park on to a fast and arrived at five past nine at Baker Street.

During the morning, we had a series of people in referred by their doctors to have metatarsal supports. Stephen was kept quite busy. Mrs Arkoft called as expected, and I agreed to remake the back of her shoe lower. Miss Irene Clunie also came and looked at the rooms and took the names of painters to do up her rooms.

I left shortly before five and met the bus at Watford Station. I was disappointed. The roof trim was not replaced. The manager said the sun roof was out of alignment and if the trim was fitted, it might make it worse. Also, the re-sprayed paintwork was in bad condition. Next door is their body works and on Saturday, they can give an estimate. I will also go and see Paddy who did the re-spray.

When I'd had supper, I quickly touched up the bits of varnish that I'd missed on the hall floor.

Peter May and I then went to the Ruislip Woods Advisory Committee. As always, we seemed to make no or little impact.

MAYDAY

Rang Martin and wished him well with the new job.

Caught the train which turned into a slow. The morning was brightened up with a 'phone call to repair a boot for Liberace, the glittering piano player. A sweet old lady with a deep voice brought it. The zip was broken. Mr Carpenter fixed it and then I took a couple of polaroid photos of it.

We had an order from an old Bell customer through Barts, and then Mrs Kiryluk, whose husband had been in the Wellington, ordered a pair of suede brogue casuals, and paid on account.

I had too much for lunch. The left overs from last night, two pieces of pizza, and a large piece of apple cake.

The shop was quite busy after lunch, with a party of Arabs to whom I sold two pairs of Greens shoes. The patient had been sent by Mona Goshen. I fitted the 3/8 cork seat pieces.

I went for a spin on the bike to the London Foot to deliver and collect adjusted shoes. Then to Tottenham Street and deliver schedules to thc Middlesex Hospital, and on to John Lewis for light bulbs, and suede dye. I got back to find we had taken another order recommended by a Dr J Mathews. He is a new Harley Street surgeon and I sent him a thank you letter.

A young man with a wheelchair came in just before we closed and made enquiries about having shoes made. He had been sent by Maxwells.

This evening, after supper, I'll collect resident subscriptions.

On Friday evening, collected eight subs and popped in at Claude Heineman and Phyl Gallagher's

02.05.81

Took the paper to the car park. Met Graham Dix. His wife is due with their second baby any day.

Cut the lawn and my dinner did not switch on as the as was not turned on. Drove in to the shop and wrote out all the contract prices. Then on to 49 Tottenham Street to load up as much rubbish and wood into the car as I could.

03.05.81

A dull overcast morning. Unloaded the car and cleaned nails and angle brackets out of the batteries. Had five of the worst pieces.

It began to rain at lunchtime. The oven was set correctly and I even had some left over for the evening. Tidied up the house. Watched telly for a few minutes when Judith and her parents arrived. We had a coffee together. I left early for the Airport to collect the family. Terminal 1 for a change. Their plane was 15 minutes late.

I watched the planes for a while from the upstairs lounge and was told that Lady Diana was taking off in a BA Trident. We read that the plane was struck by lightning, but unharmed.

04.04.81

Bank Holiday. Slept until 8.30. Had a good breakfast. Did some gardening and took the children up the road with the bikes.

In the afternoon, Hentschy and I filled insulation on to the wall of the playroom.

We ran out of rubber solution. After the children went to bed, I collected Residents Association subs in Eastbury Road.

05.05.81

Back to work. Travelled with Denis Cave. He says he has put his house on the market. He is an old misery. The post was good. Mrs Schroder confirmed her two orders with a cheque.

The Auditors from MacIntyre Hudson finished at lunch time and I gave him a pair of Greens shoes.

I went over to Tottenham Street to see the new agent and he asked if I would send the schedule of dilapidations to him. I checked with Gerard Disbrey and he agreed.

Hentschy was not feeling well. I popped over to David Thomson and collected the Christian Aid envelopes and then went on to see Chris & Lawrie. I wanted to see how to make a lowered cciling for our playroom. It looks too much work and materials, so I think we will stick to insulating the outside walls.

06.05.81

Travelled up with Betty Sewell. It looks as if the Northwood Council of Churches is heading for a bit of a storm over the Brandt Commission, The Church of England think it is too political. The Brandt Commission basically asks wealthy nations to support the poor nations.

In the shop, we had photographers the whole day. They had a lot of gear and took an hour just to set up one shot, with numerous tests and polaroids before using colour plates. It seemed to impress the customers and we took five orders. The most important were a Mr Poggart, and Dr Gough-Thomas. Bob Miller, the photographer and his assistant, Peter Chadwick, were considerate and we got on well. They hope to use the photos to sell to colour supplements, which will give us some publicity.

Rang Richard Hewgill and I will have lunch with him tomorrow at Kensington Town Hall.

07.05.81

Went to vote before I caught the train. Voted for Stephenson, Liberal this time. Of the two election blurbs through my door, his was the best. The Tory did not even bother, and he won.

We had quite a busy morning in the shop, and I went to Swinards to collect the tickets for Mr Carpenter. Then I cycled through Hyde Park and on to Kensington Town Hall to see Richard for lunch. The place he works is in a huge new place designed by Basil Spence. Very impressive with mature trees inside the courtyard.

We had lunch at a pub and I snuffled my sandies. On the way back, I went via Montpelier Street, where Kembers the shoemakers used to be, No. 4 is a dress boutique with the lease up for sale.

In the afternoon, a Mr Lundy called to have shoes made. He dictated the terms and was very particular.

I have grave doubts whether we should risk our efforts making shoes for him. McAfees have kicked him out and Mr Wark, who I rang to consult, said he was always changing his mind.

Hentschy and Martin agreed to me not making shoes for that man.

In the evening, I went to St Matthews for a Christian Aid meeting. David Thompson showed a very good film strip and the meeting was well attended.

08.05.81

Travelled up with Ron Simpson and Betty Sewell.

Had quite a shirty morning with the worst, an old lady from Wembley who was determined not to have the shoes we had made for her. She and her sisters made all sorts of claims. They left the shoes with us and I will await their claim through the court.

Mrs Childe from Queensland ordered another pair and was much more pleasant. A young man asked if a film could be made at the shop and took some shorts. We will see what they offer.

I went to see Mr Logan, our Auditor. I spent two hours with him. He juggled with the accounts to show a small loss, but to receive a refund of Corporation Tax and stock relief so that we end up with more retained profit.

Lee Golding arrived at Northwood at 8.30.

09.05.81

Hentschy went shopping while I cut the grass and Lee played with the children.

After lunch, we drove to Kew. They kept dry. Went into a part I had not seen before, Queen Charlotte's Cottage. A beautiful wood carpeted with bluebells with a path leading to a thatched cottage which we went in. It had been the Royal picnic summer house.

10.05.81

After breakfast, I took Lee by car up to the Manchester family, in Leicestershire. We left Hentschy and the children at home because Nan felt she had had a bit too much on lately.

The road was clear and we arrived at quarter to one in time for a roast beef and Yorkshire pudding lunch.

After lunch, we had a drive over to Ian's farm, so Lee could meet him and then a trip round the Vale of Beevor. The sun shone and it was warm.

On the way back, we passed an accident on the A1 near the Ram Jam Inn. Then we were held up at Sandy by a massive traffic crawl and near Hatfield we saw another accident where a caravan had come off the road.

11.05.81

Lee left for France and I went up to town on an earlier train so that she would catch her connection. During the morning, Mr Lundy's secretary 'phoned to say that his chauffeur was coming with his shoes. I said I was not prepared to work on Mr Lundy's terms, so she put him on to me. I explained I had tried to ring on Friday, but no reply. He managed again to get my adrenaline flowing. He asked who I had spoken to at McAfees. I refused to say and then the conversation closed with me, saying I found him too domineering.

Plenty of other more pleasant customers came in. Mr Deed from the landlords 'phoned to suggest our lease on Tottenham Street could be settled if we paid £500 towards the dilapidations.

I tried to ring Gerard Disbrey but he was out.

In the evening, after supper, I collected a few more subscriptions for the Residents Association.

12.05.81

Travelled up with Betty Sewell and read part of the Apocrypha. The first mention of a 'Jesus' I found the shortage in the petty cash straight away. I had missed Stephen's IOU.

I sold an old pair of shoes to an elderly lady with a swollen foot. It took at least an hour, and saw to several people in the meantime.

In the evening, I recruited the Georges as Road Stewards for the Residents Association.

13.05.81

Wednesday. Mrs Jardin came in and I could do the West End Master Bootmakers Agenda and get the Minutes typed.

In the afternoon, I went to see Miss Allen at Meckleburgh Square.

Miss Allen had discharged herself from St Pancras Hospital. She weighs only 4 stone and a friend opened the door for me. I wanted to re-measure her as the loss of weight had shrunk her feet. The poor old dear was being sick and the friend was not at all happy. We tried to ring a doctor and see if she can be put back in hospital because she was in a bad state.

I went on to Great Ormond Street Children's Hospital to deliver a pair of boots.

A lady from the film company came to look at the shop. I don't know what I am letting myself in for, or what to charge.

Dr Dale also called to see what our services are.

When I got home, Lee Golding had returned from France. We planned the rest of the days with her. I will try to get theatre tickets for CATS, a new musical, and I must also try to find a babysitter.

Lee and I went over to see our relatives, the Luddingtons, and we could have talked all night.

Hentschy was sour because I was late getting in.

14.05.81

Thursday. Cup Final today as on Saturday, West Ham and Manchester United drew. The train tonight is fairly full of football supporters.

A busy morning with Miss Burke as hopeless at sorting out the typewriter as ever.

This afternoon, we had an invasion of film people to look at the shop. They all seemed over 6ft and about 8 of them. Mrs Pichart came in just before them and seemed quite frightened by them.

I'm sure it's going to be money well earned if we let them in. They mentioned filming in the evenings and that they would ring on Monday with any propositions.

Tonight, I'll be helping with the Christian Aid collection.

15.05.81

Friday. The shop was pretty busy, especially with Arabs. The last news was that Beckett and Bird are ceasing and so I will 'phone around the surgeons and let them know that we will make appliances.

In the evening, Lee arrived to look at the shop. Maggie did the window on the theme of shoe making using her big photos.

I had managed to buy tickets to see "Annie", the musical and Hentschy drove in. Before she arrived, Lee and I could have a MacDonalds sitting in the park in Paddington Street. Weather warm and sunny.

The musical was very spectacular and we all enjoyed it, just a bit too sweet perhaps.

When we left the theatre, we were surprised to see it pouring with rain.

16.05.81

Saturday. We rang up Mum Heathman and went and collected her and brought her back to Northwood. Lee treated us to lunch at "Christians". In the afternoon, we looked at Lee's photos. Generally, extremely good. In the evening, Lee and I drove Mum H home and then went on into London to pick up a catalogue she had at No. 4 and then we had a spin to look at flood lit London.

17.05.81

Sunday. Lee packed, 'phoned Frank. Marian asked her to make a tape about Australia. Hentschy and I continued putting insulation on the wall of the playroom.

During the morning, Lee announced that her money was missing. She searched through all her things and could not find it. We cannot imagine where it had gone. I'm sure she was absent-minded and has tucked it somewhere.

We took her to the Airport in the afternoon and I'm sure she is in Singapore by now.

After the children were in bed, Hentschy and I walked down to see Mrs Lasman. It was a lovely evening and we asked her back for a chat.

18.05.81

Judith and Lynn were back from their holidays and had breakfast with us. Met Bill Price on the way down to the station. Caught a slow Baker Street and changed at Pinner on to the fast to travel with Betty Sewell.

I thought Gerald Joyce was up in the office and was surprised when Shirley called in to say he had a bout of sickness and would be in later.

We had a letter from the Citizens Advice Centre about Mrs Reynolds. I expect we will have a court case over it.

I went over to Lawries to buy some golf soles. We took quite five orders in the morning and another two in the afternoon.

It was pretty wet all day. After four, I went out again to Tottenham Street and left a key for Mrs Pellegrini so the drain could be done again. Then on to Bentick Street to see Miss Birchill. 84. Proprietor of Beckett & Bird.

She confirmed that she was going to voluntarily liquidate her firm. Partly her age, partly the new contract. Partly, lack of staff. I offered to buy her interests and possibly take on staff, but she said she would discuss it with her Auditors. My course of action will be to 'phone round the doctors.

Hentschy and I watched telly on Monday and saw "The Thomas Crown Affair", film. I have always enjoyed it.

19.05.81

I had just got out of bed and Martin rang. He realised his insurance was not valid for business use. I decided to write to the Commercial Union and deliver the letter by hand in Harrow. I wrote the letter on the train and then came straight back to collect the car and drive up to Northampton. I met Mr Swan when I left the train at Northwood and asked him to give the builders a message to call.

The car ran well up the motorway. Notices saying delays possible until November were disconcerting. At the Watford Gap service station, I turned out through the staff exit and then it was only 1.5 miles to Long Buckby.

I asked the way to Frank Eyre from a milk lady with a horse drawn cart. Frank Eyre is above the Community Centre but very badly signposted. I met Mrs Ross (Trisch). She had white hair and looked very pregnant. Due 9th July. Her office was a tip. Bags of rubbish giving off a right smell. Marmite cases under her desk and gross disorder.

She is a pleasant enough person, but it was rather cheerless and cold and I was glad to leave for the Saxon Hotel in the centre of Northampton.

The Footwear Training Board had organised a course in Marketing. It started at 12 with Professor Gordon Wills telling us what it is all about. We had a buffet lunch and I met the Directors of Trickers. I may be able to get more of a dialogue going with them.

The afternoon dealt with a case study on marketing. How Not To Do It and then How To Do Better.

I also made contact with the MD of Hawkins who make riding and climbing boots that could be a useful contact.

The trip home went well. The evening was mild and dry and after supper, Hentschy and I had a pleasant walk down Green Lane to Rickmansworth Road and back up Maxwell and Murray Road.

20.05.81

As I left the house in a torrential thunderstorm, I helped Miss Leader out of Dr Baker's car. She was the Headmistress of St. Helens School. Caught the fast Aldgate, so I should be in the shop by 8.45. Later on I'll go with Hentschy to a Royal Forestry Society meeting at Kenwood.

Before I left, I measured up a lady for met pads sent by Mr Scott. There were about 20 people at the meeting and the man who took us round spoke very well and gave us a good impression of the problems under which he worked.

Hentschy and I had a lovely lunch on a bench overlooking the house and lake. The AGM was quite lively and it seems a drive is on for new members.

Back at the shop, it was busy and we took a new order just before it closed.

Residents Association Roads Stewards meeting tonight. It was well attended and Fergus Robertson was a much better Chairman. It seems the tennis club is a problem.

21.05.81

A busy morning with plenty of orders to catch up with to book from yesterday.

Miss Burke also came in and it was a struggle to get the letter to the Citizens Advice Centre written. It was about a Mrs Reynolds.

Just as I was about to eat my lunch, Tina, the physiotherapist, 'phoned, asking me to come and see Mrs Charles' shoes. Gerald Joyce showed me pictures of Agadir. I left at quarter to one and saw Mrs Charles and agreed to shorten her shoes. Then on to Middlesex Hospital and Miss Wheeler. She seemed chatty enough and I collected three pairs of repairs.

Then on to Egeli's to see if he would like some lasts. I sheltered from the rain there, then cycled back to Tottenham Street. 'Phoned up Barry Sullivan who was not there, so talked to Kevin.

Had a 'phone call from the National Theatre asking for Lasts as props. £4 a pair. 36 pairs wanted. The Actor from the film company had another look at Mustapha.

'Phoned up Disbrey our solicitor re 49 Tottenham Street and then Mr Deed to conclude the lease and tenancy next Friday.

Mr Carpenter had a busy session at the London Foot Hospital. 4 orders and several adaptions.

We had a quote from the builders to put in a false ceiling in the playroom. £200+ They will start next Wednesday.

22.05.81

Friday. Not a single order, but plenty of activity. I left at 4.30 to go home and fetch the car. When I arrived home, I had several calls. Mr Becker needed some Lasts, Mr Lobb wanted to read a letter he had written to Prince Charles, Mr Bryson wanted confirmation about using the Northwood Council of Churches on the notepaper to ask speakers for a meeting on Brandt.

I drove in with the car to clear out the rest of the things from Tottenham Street and came back with a load to 4 Paddington Street, and then a load of wood to Carew Lodge. I can use it to make a sandpit.

23.05.81

We drove up to Martin at Keighley. Left at 11.30 and ate our lunch on the road. Arrived at 4 just as another family was leaving.

It was bright and sunny and once we had put the kids to bed, we had a walk up the road to the town Lee and I had visited during the heavy snow.

24.05.81

Sunday. The sun shone and rather than go to church or meeting , we took Carolyn and Martin in our car to Bolton Abbey and then walked up to the strid. 4 miles. It was further than we had expected and so we decided I should go back to the road and fetch the car.

We had walked through beautiful mature woods, carpeted with bluebells and flowering wild garlic. At the road, I tried to thumb a lift and jogged down the road. To my luck and astonishment, a police panda car stopped and gave me a lift down to Bolton Avenue car park.

I drove back to the Strid car park and arrived just as they did. We got back for a good lunch and after lunch, we packed Liz, Jason, Carolyn, Martin, Hentschy, Michael, Jenny and me, yes 8 of us, into our Beetle and went to Haworth. It was pouring with rain when we arrived. The lower car park was full, so we drove up to another one where we could park. We walked over to the Bronte Museum, where there was a queue to go in, so we walked down the High Street under our umbrellas to the railway station. As we walked over the footbridge, we saw a train in the station and watched it leave for Keighley. We paid to have a walk round the station yard with plenty of old locos, including L89 London Transport saddle tank engine from Neasden.

In the evening, a local GP from Keighley popped in. He had been in the year above Martin at Leeds.

25.05.81

After breakfast, Martin mowed the grass. He seized up the neighbour's Flymo and finished the job with another neighbour's electric rotary. I had a good session weeding his front garden.

After lunch, we loaded up and left about 3.30. We drove down the motorway through some heavy rain and at Northampton turned off when we saw a solid jam ahead. We went down the A5 as far as Dunstable and re-joined the M1 there.

The house was fine, but the garden was waterlogged.

26.05.81

I took a pair of Lasts in from the shed up to town, but left the drawing behind. Maggie and Mr Wilson are on holiday this week. We had a busy day with two American repeat customers ordering and one from Bermuda. The film company collected the props and I fixed the Ascot in the kitchen with a new washer. 20p instead of a call out plumber. John Winfield on the train.

In the evening, the three new Bible Bashers called to see the rooms. A tall one called Louise from Watford, middle one called Liz from Pitlochry and a short one called Karen from Port Madoc.

Derek Curtler also called for the proposal form for Martin.

27.05.81

Met the charming Canadian called Ray in Eastbury Road. Went on the fast Baker Street and saw Betty Sewell. Kept busy with people all morning. Mrs Jardin came in and typed the West End Master Bookmaker's balance sheet and did a lot of filing.

I went over to London Foot Hospital and then saw Miss Wheeler at the Middlesex. They were on the point of moving back to their old offices.

A rep from Rentokill came in to see if we had Cockroaches. The greengrocers had a problem. I decided against a yearly contract and bought an aerosol instead.

Rain again this evening. Sanne rang to say Tante Marie from Leipzig, would be coming on Saturday to stay for a week.

28.05.81

I found some mushrooms in the garden last night and cooked them for breakfast. They were alright. Used the fast Aldgate being a bit later. When I arrived at the shop, Mrs Hyman had brought her husband's shoes back for dovetailed heels to be put on and a girl from the film company was waiting for a shoemaker's apron and a lady's shoe Last. Miss Burke arrived and I had a few letters for her. Mr Langley Pope from Wiesbaden came in and ordered another pair of shoes. I went down to see Dr Hatchick for an anti-hay fever jab.

Mr Maguire was glad I delivered his remade shoes. The left one seemed fine now but the right was a bit tight over the joint. The London Clinic had asked me to fit a patient on Room 333. His son objected to the price and said he would buy the shoes himself. I was not sorry because the old man had only one leg and it was a typical Arab foot, short and very wide.

I rang the employers Protection Society for advice on how to retire Miss Burke. They suggested eight weeks pay in lieu of notice.

During the evening, Hentschy and I papered the lowered ceiling in the playroom. It looks good.

29.05.81

Friday. With Maggie on holiday, I seemed to be running about a fair bit. One new St Thomas's patient in the morning.

At 2.30, a lady came to hire some tools and a cutting board for a commercial, to be returned on Tuesday. I went over to see Mr Deed to wind up our tenancy at 49 Tottenham Street. It took just half an hour. I went straight back to Tottenham Street and gave Mrs Pelligrini her shoes which we had made open toe. I had a quick drink with her and her daughter and explained a Tax refund to her. At the Middlesex Appliance Office, Miss Wheeler was in her new den, with a soggy carpet caused by a leaking radiator in the nearly installed central heating. She was her usual shirty self. Next call, Burket, the ironmongers to collect keys they had cut and a gallon of meths for Mustapha. Back at the shop, a new customer was holding forth, but at least she bought some Solidus Shoes.

The film crew turned up at quarter to five and I let them get cracking. We opened the cellar flaps and they set up in the basement. There were about 30 people. They brought their own generator which was set up by the Baker and Oven, with cable running in through the cellar flaps.

I watched most of the actual filming with Carols sitting in Mustapha's chair and acting very well. He was shown cutting a heel lift and putting some red shoes in a box. The film company paid £138 for the privilege and left about 9 o'clock.

30.05.81

We went to the Airport to collect Tante Marie. She was on time and looking about the same as last year. She will stay for a week. After lunch, I cut the grass. It was very high and heavy. During the afternoon, we watched as No. 1 Carew Road was being demolished, and Michael even had a ride on the bulldozer. He was scared at first but then loved it.

31.05.81

Sunday. I went to Meeting on my own. It was a bit of peace and it was full of the old stalwarts. I will see if I can help Margaret Wheeler's campaign.

After lunch, the sun shone and I planted some beans, lay in the deckchair, drank iced coffee, went round to No. 1 and met John from 14 Eastbury Road. Hentschy sheared the D clip from the lawn mower, and we started to make a sandpit. Once the children were in bed, we could finish the job.

01.06.81

The weather is lovely for a change. Hentschy lost her temper with Jenny at breakfast and with shouting, slapping and screaming, I was glad to go to London. I rang later and Hentschy sounded ashamed of herself, as she ought to.

There was a steady stream of small jobs all day but only one new order from a Mrs Sainsbury.

I spent some time finding out how to get our cellar pavement flaps repaired. I will have them welded and then re-glazed.

It is hot and sticky in the train this evening. The first really warm day this year.

I met Bruce at Harrow and slipped back to his house to buy some layer bits. Hentschy was sour because I was later getting in.

I cut some hedge and looked at No. 1. A lot of the cover had been cut away.

02.06.81

During the night, there was a torrential thunderstorm with hours of sheet lightening. The children slept through it. In the morning, we could see the garden was waterlogged.

Travelled up with Betty Sewell. We worked out an agenda for this evening's Standing Committee.

We seemed to have a fair few complainers during the day. Mrs Sass, Mr Phillips etc. etc. Life would be too simple if they didn't. George Deliss a shoemaker with a shop in Beauchamp Place Knightsbridge, came over for some golf spikes to put in shoes he was making.

Miss Burke was also in and peed on the floor.

In the afternoon, I popped into John Bell and Croydon and left a few cards. Delivered Ester Gartner's repaired boots at the Middlesex Hospital and admired the new office.

Collected the three old coats from 49 Tottenham Street and that should be the last time I call in.

Maggie is back from her holiday in Paris. She was in a happy frame of mind.

A photographer from New York 'phoned to ask if he could take pictures in the shop and use our name in a magazine. He will come tomorrow.

03.06.81

A warm sunny day. We had a good number of cheques in today.

I popped over to the London Clinic to bring some shoes to a Pakistani who had a shortening. He was over anxious and I had to ask him to stop telling me my job.

In the afternoon, I had a meeting of the West End Master Bootmakers in the room on the third floor. Hentschy's cake was appreciated and the tea seemed to go down well.

04.06.81

A quiet morning. Went over to UCH and heard Mr Smith's shoes had been found. What a relief. Popped in to see about the key that did not work.

Had a 'phone call from Clarks shoes re John Locke made to order shoes. Would we be their central London agent? I think it is very promising.

In the evening, I had a clear out in the safe while I waited for Hentschy and Tante Marie to arrive. We then went for a meal at the Baker & Oven.

05.06.81

A quiet morning again. In the afternoon, it was busier. I went over to see Miss Burke and retired her. It was not a pleasure. I brought a bottle of sherry and that sweetened the pill, as did a cheque for £450 i.e. six weeks' pay and five weeks holiday and the promise of a telly.

I went on to Westminster Hospital and then Miss Peters. She had lost 7 stone and her boots were too big.

In the evening, I cut more grass.

06.06.81

Saturday. As always with the family, it took ages to set out of the house. It was 11.30 before we got into the car and then dumped our old newspapers at the car park. We went on to Gavin's and bought honey and various other things and then on to Syon Park. It was almost deserted in the gardens and we had our picnic in the conservatory.

In the nearby nursery we bought an Angelica plant.

07.06.81

Tante Marie left from Heathrow and we left the house at 9 to get her there in time. A Hostess escorted her to the plane.

On the way back, we stopped at the Canal on the Stockley Road and went for a walk and picked elder flowers.

After lunch, I cut the grass again and Hentschy cleared next to the shed and the children played in the sandpit.

Once they were in bed, we prepared the Elderberry sparkling wine.

08.06.81

A quiet morning. I booked an order for Miss Kirraine. After lunch, I went to the Business to Business exhibition. I cycled there against the wind. It was full. I went in for every free competition, giving my name and address in all directions.

I don't think I gained very much.

Mr Cole came to look at the cellar flaps. We agreed to replace the left one with a metal flap and repair the right one.

A 'bingo' holiday

Mr William Wilson, who works as a pattern cutter/clicker for James Taylor & Sons, London bespoke shoemakers, and his wife will take their holiday this year in Los Angeles in early April. They always enjoy their holidays, I am told, but this one will be particularly exciting and enjoyable – after all, it will cost them nothing. It was the bingo prize won by Mr Wilson last week and with it went £600 in cash and $100 spending money.

Mr Wilson is 77 and still working, his employer, Mr Peter Schweiger, told me.

Tuesday, 11 August 1981

Having lost my last journal last Friday at the Beau Sejour leisure centre at Guernsey, I will just note that latest.

We went for a holiday with Volke and Sanne to the Wellesley hotel on Guernsey. 10 of the 14 days were sunny. We were the only guests some of the time and hired a mini

Metro to travel with. We went twice to Herm and once to Sark.

Yesterday was the first day back. All seem to have run well. And a lot of work but not many orders. The local W1 post has also been on strike.

Today I took our car to Moss Motors in Watford for servicing. At the shop I was faced with a mountain of mail which had at last come through.

The shop was busy in the morning with several people ordering supports and an Arab man for shoes through the Corfton clinic. We will have to find more seating for peak times. We had a man recommended by Mr Winchester sent for a corset. We sent him to John Bell and Croydon who sent him to Donald Rose.

I called in on Mr Roberts at Donald Rose and collected some cards. I had a busy time on the bike calling at the London Foot hospital, the Middlesex hospital, S. Allen and Co. to order trees for Mr Rosenberg. While I was there I saw a pair of riding boots for the Queen made by Maxwells with trees and brass plates with her name on it.

The car has passed the M. O. T. Not bad for a 1972 V. W. Orange beetle. It has to be on top form for her trip to East Germany next week.

Wednesday 12th August 1981

Another hot sunny day. Stephen Blakley came in with a tax code. He will start in September to learn last fitting. I'm sure his services as a chiropodist will also be in demand. It was a pleasant day with a steady flow of contented

166

customers. It must be the sun. Only three orders though the rest were for repairs and supports. I seem to be unable to shake off a rotten cough and throat. I felt quite ill after lunch and slept for about half an hour on the couch upstairs. I only went out for a short while to give a film in and see Graham Dix at Barclays bank at the corner of Baker Street.

Thursday 13th August 1981

Another hot day. Moderate volume of business. Mrs Schroeder ordered another pair of shoes in black lizzard and payed with the order. The tape recorder broke down so I wrote my letters in long hand for Shirley Joyce to type. One was for Lobbs concerning the shoes we want to give as a wedding present to Prince Charles.

Maggie, the receptionist, Dial 1999 this afternoon when she saw a man and woman in the street with a bag over her head. I later saw the woman being led by two policeman back to a house in Devonshire Street. Maybe she was a nut who had escaped from a nursing home.

I rang David Price at John Locke he said he would ring back tomorrow whether we would have the agency for their shoes.

Thursday 14th of August 1981.

Another scorcher. Kenneth good came in to give me and half yearly report. The morning was taken up with Mr Kavanna who was recommended to us by Colin Knockholt, for a pair of shoes to accommodate his cosmetic caliper.

After lunch I went over to the Middlesex hospital and to meet Mr Egeli to give him a note to help him with his Visa for Turkey.

Then I went on 295 Piccadilly to see two films made by Concern. My brother Martin was a volunteer with them 1974 - 1976.

One of the films was called "Any more for crutches" and what about the Cheshire home in Zimbabwe. It gave me the idea that the Training Board manual could be adapted for relief agencies or the textbook, "Where there is no shoemaker". There is a book called "Where there is no Doctor". I also met Mr Rossi, the Minister of Health and was able to tell him my thoughts on the DHSS.

15th of August 1981

We took Sanne and Volker with our car to Hatfield. On the way back we took the wrong turning and went up the M 10. It was a long detour.

We had a leisurely day in the garden with the children. Hentschy was very fed up with Michael. On Friday he had left the water overflowing from the wash-basin. Soaked his carpet and brought the corner of the dining room ceiling down. Then on Saturday morning he dropped a full bottle of milk on the kitchen floor.

Sunday

Hentschy did not feel well and stay in bed. The children and I made her breakfast. It was fairly heavy going with

Michael and in the afternoon I had a sleep in a deckchair while Hentschy played with them.

In the evening we filled in the forms for East Germany.

Monday

Sunny. Plenty of repairs. Gerald Joyce had the day off. Two orders. One from Keith Cole and the other from the mother of Mrs Rogers. A good day for banking. Sean Taylor of Police Five was at the Baker and Oven. In the evening I cut the lawn and collected cheques from Ron Turner for Elizabeth Vonberg.

Tuesday 18th August 1981 -18 8 81

It can be written upside down, mirror etc, an interesting date. I gave Betty Sewell the posters for the Northwood Council of Churches. It was fairly quiet. I went over to the London foot hospital with boots for Dr Graham and to the Middlesex hospital with Dennis Fort's.

In the afternoon a vain American woman came in recommended by Mr Scott. I doubt if we will actually make for her. She was going to look for a picture of what she wants.

This evening there is a Frithcare meeting at Barbara Brandenburger's. We will learn what is happening to the park and the other plans for the area. With a rep. from the tennis club and the area planner together, a workable idea for access to the park can evolve. The club could have planning permission to build on their redundant court in exchange for a shared use of the drive as access to the park.

Wednesday 19th of August 1981

We got up at 6.30 so that we could finish packing the car and be away to Harwich. We had to stop at Ware where Jenny was sick as a dog. We arrived at Harwich and then we ran round the town looking for the Prince Hamlet. It was very badly signposted. We had arrived in good time but the Hamlet left nearly an hour late, for a reason we never found out. We had a cabin with two bunk beds, to the delight of the children who could share the ladder so they could both sleep on the top. We had a picnic lunch and then a walk round.

At the kiosk we had a choc ice on a stick. We met some other little children in the playroom. One boy had a terrible black eye. He had fallen onto the corner of a kerb.

There was quite a swell and we felt very tired and went to bed at 6:30. We slept well on the swell in spite of the smell of people unwell.

20th of August 1981

We woke and got up just an hour before we landed. The car was loaded and we watched on deck with the music blaring as we came into the dock at St Pauli. There were not many cars or passengers so we could disembark quickly. We have no problems with customs and were with Sanne by 9.30. Hentschy drove. A good breakfast was waiting for us and we were happy to see Sanne again. When we packed again and drove to Hertie, the department store, to buy a pocket camera as we had left ours at home. We found an Agfamatic for 99 DM and a new mac for Michael. Then Sanne guided us to the E. German border at Horst. We made our farewells and then drove to the controls. We were surprised that petrol coupons were not available and we were told we could buy petrol with DDR money. The inspection of our car and luggage was a formality and the lady was interested in a newspaper cutting about the DDR so we gave it to her.

Hentschy drove very carefully to observe the speed limits. We followed the main road to Berlin, but turned off to head towards Stendal. A police car coming towards us indicated we should stop. It turned round and came up to us. They wanted to know where we were going. Michael happily chatted them up and we went on our way.

We arrived at Stendal and asked several people for Karnipp which we found without much trouble. The Fischers live in a very trim and freshly decorated little house in a tiny lane. *Gretschen is a cousin of Hentschy's on her mother's side. Gretschen's first husband had been killed in WW2. she married Fred who was thought of as simple. He had once had a thunderbolt of lightening in his trousers.* We were made very welcome and shown up to her bedroom which one had a large double bed and a table and chairs in it. We had sat for a long time in the car so I took the children for a walk in the town. A busy street with no cars. Some shops were closed for summer holidays.

We had a good supper for the children first and Michael slept in the double bed and Jenny was in the separate room. After a supper of cheese and salad gherkins we had a bottle of wine and slept well.

21st of August 1981

It was showery. I went straight after breakfast to register with the police. I didn't have to wait long and it was all done quickly and courteously. On the way back I saw that the wedding was being held at the Rathaus. I fetched the children and saw the bride and groom unpeg three rows of washing which were really presents. They then cut a log with a crosscut saw and threw sweets and coins to the crowd. Michael and Jenny managed to get their share. I took a few photos before they drove off.

Fred took us for a walk. He is very ill with diabetes and could not really tell us what we were looking at. We went into the Dome which was in good condition. The choir stalls were very old.

Lunch of roulladen, potatoes cucumber salad and gravy. Bottled cherries for afters. It was pouring down so we were happy to go for a walk with the car round the town and then out to Rockau where Hentschy born. We just drove through the village and out again. We returned via Borstal and saw plenty of barracks and helicopters. We fed and put the children to bed and then have a cosy supper. Later on I went for a walk with Fred and found a dance going on at the local hotel.

22nd of August 1981

After breakfast we packed and made our farewells. We drove to Leipzig via Magdeburg. Somehow we landed on the wrong road and it took rather longer than we had hoped. We found the Autobahn. It was pretty full and quite a lot of BRD (West German) cars. When we went towards Leipzig

172

though it was much emptier. The street map helped us find Tante Marie very quickly. She lives in the flat on the third floor in a large old house. The furniture was lovely and she had a large sitting room with plenty of plants. We could look down on the street. To one side were some containers and people put their rubbish in and others took it out. A regular free jumble sale.

The children were very restless and I was very glad when we drove round to Tante Marie's son Wolfgang. We were very impressed with his flat. All mod cons including colour telly. Immaculate decoration throughout and tastefully furnished. He and his wife Rugina kindly put us up in their bedroom. They slept in their son's room. He is away on holiday.

23rd of August 1981

After a very good breakfast we went by tram to the city centre. We walked around looking at the shops and old town Hall. The St Thomas's church has a very steep roof. We popped into a cafe and had coffee, and ices for the children. We wanted to return to the flat by train. The main station is huge with 26 platforms. Being Sunday however there were not so many trains so we went and just caught a tram back. Tante Marie was not there yet so Wolfgang and I drove round to fetch her, twice.

In the afternoon we went to the zoo. The admission was cheap and people flocked to it. Plenty of Russian uniforms. It was on pre war lines with most of the animals in cages. The monkeys gave a lot of entertainment and so did the elephants. There were also some stalks and lions and tigers etc. Well well worth going to again. The children also had a go on a pony drawn roundabout, and on pony back in a ring. Jenny cried because it wobbled! But got used to it eventually.

24th of August 1981. Dad's birthday in 1908

We spent the morning all going shopping in Leipzig. We bought toys and underwear and pyjamas for Michael. We queued for a basket to get in. That way the shop was not so full. I invited our hosts out for lunch. The first place we tried was very full with a big queue so we went to the inter-hotel. There was only a short queue. I had steak and champinons with rot kraut and chips. It was excellent. Was rather in different and it was half an hour until we could have ice creams. For seven people the meal cost 125 marks. Which compares with a meal at home for that standard.

We went back to a shop to buy plates where the salesman told the people where to go. We nearly went to, but put up with his stroppiness to actually buy them. We drove onto the Slacht Denkmahl. It was a massive monument to a battle on 18 October 1813 where the French under Napoleon were defeated. We went into the vast dome. Michael's noise echoed forever it seemed.

We went on for coffee to Tante Marie, and enjoyed Leipziger kuchen. I took the children to a nearby park. Some children asked if we if the children spoke Russian! When I said English they ran away. We went back with Tante Marie to Wolfgang's and later bathed the children who were very dirty. They had enjoyed seeing the Sandman on the telly.

25th of August 1981

We had called in on Tante Marie first before we were guided by Manfred onto the Autobahn to head for Dresden and Hoyerswerda. On the way we stopped for lunch at a service station. We had duck and rot kohl followed by ice cream. I did the driving and we left the autobahn at Bautzen. In the villages the surfaces were very rough which slowed the cars well.

In Hoyerswerda we asked a couple of people the way and then suddenly Heinz Aussner was in front of us with his car and could guide us. They live in the fifth floor of a block with views over the car park to other blocks. It was quite a puff to lug our suitcases up. The new flat is full of familiar furniture from the other place. Heinz and I went to park the cars after coffee and then to look for potatoes. The local place was full of a big queue so we drove over to where Uta and her and her family live it was a very smart affair and her two children have a nice playroom. We had a pleasant evening chatting and drinks drinking wine with pineapple.

Renate Aussner

26th of August 1981

After breakfast we had a look at the Alt Stadt and had a good look and and walk. We found the museum and animal park and looked at the ponies. I then tried to find the old flat where the Aussners used to live. It was not easy but I managed. On the way back we nearly went the wrong way up a one-way street and then we had a job to find the new flat.

We had a good lunch of stuffed peppers. Heinz came back from work and Renata stayed at the flat while we went to the old town of Bautzen. The old shops and houses have been redecorated and made into a pedestrian precinct. The large church was also open and shared by the Protestant and Catholic's. A wonderful example of a good and your use of the building.

On the road to Bautzen we went to a little village where a man had a hobby building models of dinosaurs. It was not a very big garden but cleverly landscaped with ponds and a Windmill and interesting plants. For tea we had iced coffee in a hotel in Bautzen and then drove back to Hoyerwerda to visit Uta and her young family and have supper.

27th of August 1981

It poured down in the morning as we drove to visit Edith Sofke in Konigstein.

We found our way reasonably well. The scenery was spectacular and we found her home without difficulty. We had wanted to take her out to lunch but as Konigstein is a tourist town, Edith had prepared lunch, pork and rote Kohl followed by apfel moouse.

We then went up to the castle. The weather improved and we had grand views. The railway was busy and Michael sang "Toot toot tot die Eisenbahn". We had seen a steam train on the way. There was plum cake at the cafe and Jenny made a fuss and had a smack. We had some very lovely presents and laughed a lot at the talking budgie.

We lost our way several times on the way back to Hoyerswerda. Ulrike was not yet back to our surprise and then after five minutes she was there. We had a good boozy evening and hit the hay after midnight.

28 August 1981

Hentschy packed and the sun shone so Ulrike took us to the Tierpark. We also took a neighbours child and some bread. The Zoo was better than the big Leipzig one in that the animals have more room and the layout was more imaginative. There were three lion cubs. We felt we could not stay too long although we had an ice cream and could watch sculptors from seven countries being filmed at an exhibition. There was a good lunch waiting for us and we made our farewells. We found the road to the Autobahn near Dresden with very slow crawling Russian army lorries. Once we reached the motorway things improved and we reached Markneukirchen with out too much trouble. In the town we asked a few people the way and saw Tante Liessel first sitting up at the window of the house. Her son Johannes is an engraver and his wife Irmgard had a lovely cafe clutch waiting for us. The only snag was the smelly loo which was just a hole otherwise we were in a lovely setting in an old house full of character and Hentschel family history. Our bedroom has a wash basin and an adjoining room for Michael to sleep in. Johannes gave us a tour of the workrooms and Michael became an instant engraver and engineer.

29 August 1981

After a good nights sleep and breakfast we drove with your Johannes to Klingenberg to the police station to have an exit visas put in our passports. It did not take long. Klingenburg is a town where they make mouth organs, but only for export. We drove onto a ski jump set in a valley with spruce forest all around. Went on to a large restaurant directly on the Czech border and then back through a very large forest. We called in on some friends who make violins and guitars. They showed us round their workshops and were very friendly.

We had rouladen for lunch with bottled strawberries for afters. To shake our dinner down we had a walk through the town and saw their other garden. On the way back we had a tour of the Music Museum. It was hard work to keep the children quiet but it was full of demonstrations. Sabina another cousin and was there for coffee.

In the evening we knocked back a couple of bottles of sect and talked about the politics and family photos. They also have an old-fashioned musical box with 30 discs including the Radedski march, Silent night, and old Vienna waltz.

30 August 1981 Sunday

Johannes made me a brass door plate and engraved my Swiss Army penknife, which I still have, and Jenny's bracelet and necklace and Hentschy had her watch engraved as well. Then the children went and played with the other children along the lane at the back. In the afternoon we washed up a lovely dinner service with the monogram A H from Angelica's grandmother. The sun shone and we played in the garden and then had a kaffeeklatsch with the cousin and her mother. We had a walk with cousin Lisle in her wheelchair and visited the swimming pool which was built in 1936 and looked as if it was as original. The general area it was very much better than the others we have seen may be because these were more private firms and caring people.

31 August 1981 Monday

We packed up all the goodies and make our farewells with tears. We left Markneukirchen at 10:30 and reached the dreaded border at 2 o'clock. There seemed to be very little control. we just opened our presents, back seat and engine and handed our passports in. Half an hour and that was it. The car hummed up the Autobahn to Hamburg. Seven hours and over 600 km.

Sanne was not in when we arrived and we fetchd the key from Frau Galtz. She arrived an hour later just in time to say good night to the children. She brought Oma from Wahlstedt. Oma is very senile and repeats and questions all the time.

1 9 1981 Tuesday

Mummy had another lady to look after her for a while called Sister Gertrude. She arrived at 8:30 and made a very good impression. The weather was good so we went to the Hagenbeck Zoo. On the way we bought some rolls and ham for our picnic lunch. The zoo was beautifully landscaped and the animals werc in good condition. We went into the dolphinarium after our picnic and got the got there early. The children were very excited as we waited. Then a trainer came and explained about the sea lions and the dolphins. Three sea lions alone balanced beachballs on their noses, a dolls umbrella and a light trident. Three Dolphins took their place and talked and danced. They did many things such as jumping through hoops, standing on their heads and tales and playing football. Then another dolphin did a double somersault and swam on his back waving bye, bye. It was a very good show.

We followed more numbers to more of the animals and then spent a lot of time at the playground. The big slides were the best thing. Jenny bruised her chin on one. We left later in the afternoon and bathed, fed and bedded the children.

2 9 1981

We took the car to Barmbeck station and then the U Bahn to the Landungsbrucker. There we went on a boat down the Elbe to where all ships leaving and coming to Hamburg are greeted. Picnic on a nearby beach. It was deserted and reasonably warm. Three large ships passsed going down on the tide. One was the Esso Warwickshire so the English National anthem was played. We walked in land to Wedel where we rang Elke Herzberg. She came with her car and brought us to her home for coffee and cake. The children played with Lego on a table in the garden.

The S bahn brought us back for supper with the Hafe-Ullmans came later they gave Michael an abicus with a hundred counters. Jenny had beads to thread on a string and I had a top and whip to play with.

3 9 81

The weather was clear and sunny. We went to the shoemaker's wholesaler and bought some rasps and knives.

Hentschy also bought some dresses at Karstadt. We had chicken soup for lunch. I had a sleep after lunch and then we drove to Wahlstedt to Angelica's brother's family. We sat in the sun and had lovely cream cakes. Peter came back from work later. He looks ill due to his gallstones and is having an operation in three weeks time.

4 9 81

We bought a day ticket for the underground and went to a large park called Planten and Blumen where we spent a couple of hours at large playground. Had a picnic lunch and left at three and took the S bahn to the new home of Elsbeth Wolf. She was a colleague of Hentschy's and still teaches. she lives in Wohltor in a new house on freshly laid out estate close to the station. The weather was lovely and warm so we could sit in the garden and drink coffee and also play with the children on the grass under the trees.

It was quite a long train journey back to the flat. In the evening I went out alone to the Reeperbahn. It was amazing how blatant the whores solicited and how quickly they lost interest when I said I had no money. I had a long walk about and was shown into all sorts of clubs and shows only to leave after I refuse to pay, pleading poverty.

5 9 81 Saturday

It was another lovely day. We wanted to go to the Lunerberger Heide with Sanne and Mami. We knew it would take an age to get out of the house, so I went to the playground next door for an hour or so with the children. We left eventually and I drove Sanne's Volvo with Mami sitting in front, and the two children with Sanne and Hentschy in the back. Sudemuhlen was the destination. It was part of a nature reserve the actual mill was now a restaurant and hotel. The car park was overflowing so we drove back to a deserted layby with a bench and had our picnic there. Then we went for a walk through the actual Heath.

Juniper and Heather were the main vegetation. It was very pretty almost like a graveyard in places. Beehives were set up in batteries with thatched roofs over them.

6 9 81

20734 on the clock at Wachtel Str. Hamburg. Left at 11 and arrived at Vlisslingen Netherlands at 8 in the evening. A very pleasant ship and smooth crossing.

7 9 81

We have landed. Michael left his Peter Rabbit and blanket in the cabin. Only discovered it once we had driven through immigration, but before we reached customs. I parked and Hentschy went back to the ship. Luckily she found it.

As we had some excess wine we declared it and promptly were the last in the queue. The customs officer was apologetic about charging us £4 duty for the wine. The drive home was slow. 3 hours via Dartmouth Tunnel and North circular road.

Relieved to find the house and garden in good shape. We unloaded the car and after a late breakfast I bought a monthly season for £46. and went into town. The shop had been quiet with no major problems. I read through the post and caught up with things.

The children were in the bath when I got home. after supper Hentschy and I cut up the rose hips and took the pips out to make rose hip jelly.

8 9 81

On the radio as we were getting up I heard that a derailment at Harrow on the Hill had disrupted trains from Northwood. Hentschy drove me to Harrow and I caught a fast Aldgate and arrived earlier than usual. The shop was fairly busy from the start, with an order from Mrs Simon for Solidus shoes. During the morning David Price from John Locke rang and asked me to contact Alan Drew. Maybe I will undertake to sell his shoes on a private basis and not on the NHS contract, if Drews get permission from the NHS.

Rob de Jong, a dutch shoemaker called in. He is on a contract in the Sudan but was sorting out job possibilities for next year.

I went over to see a Mrs Bearing in the King Edward V11th Hospital and brought her some Drew shoes. She was not able to give them a go as she needed a larger size.

The trains are back to normal this evening. I also had a call from Ann Powell of the Gazette about the park.

In the evening Hentschy made rose hip jam which turned out well. Such a distinct smell and taste. I sorted out my bills and wrote a couple of letters.

9 9 81

Good weather again. Met Betty Sewell who told me about the fire in her flat. An electrical fault on her cooker caused three thousand pounds worth of damage.

I sold two pairs of Solidus shoes. One pair was to an Arab lady who needed a new artificial limb and I arranged a consultation at Vessa limb fitting centre, Roehampton. The other pair was for a Mrs Syble MacGregor wife of the chairman of British Steel Corp. She has very thin feet.

In the afternoon I went on a short round with my bike. Delivered a pair of foot supports to 1 Harley St., The Middlesex Hospital, Allens the Tree makers to have some lasts copied, The London Foot Hospital to deliver repairs. I also called in at the Royal National Orthopaedic Hospital where I said Hallo, but saw no chance of work flowing back. I went on to see Mrs Baring who then bought a pair of Dru shoes that fitted.

10 9 81

Another sunny day. Michael Williams came in and ordered another pair, but I will have to wait to get the official order before we start because the hospital were sticky last time. I dictated a lot of letters for Shirley Frost after lunch. Spoke to Irene Clunie's sister who circularises hairdressers. That could be worth trying.

I cycled over to Lawries in Seymour St. for Vibram soles. A new stock had just arrived and was being checked so all I could get were a pair of heels.

When I returned to the shop I sent the patching machine to Kaufman's in Dalston by taxi to be repaired. Mr Carpenter went to his clinic at the London Foot Hospital. He came back with one new order for Miss Klein for whom we made shoes for in 1974. He even found the lasts.

Maggie borrowed the orange bike and Mike her boy friend came to collect it.

11.9 81

Met Betty Sewell and Mary again on the train.

Mr Rivkin called in to order two more pairs of boots size 18! One private and paid for in advance and one pair on the NHS. The sewing machine was returned by taxi. Mrs Jardin (former typist) phoned to say her husband had a job French polishing in Northwood. They will call in at home in Northwood at noon.

After lunch I cycled and delivered two pairs of boots to the Hon Hugh Astor of the Times. His house keeper took them in at his town house in Culross St. Mayfair. Cyril Castle, the tailor in Conduit St. was my next call. His shoes fitted and he then ordered a second pair and paid a deposit. I called in at Berolina travel to enquire about going to Berlin. It should be quite easy. At the Middlesex Hospital I delivered shoes for Dr. Burgess and collected orders. I popped into see Mr Bodington, the manager at Babers of Oxford St, and then bought two photo albums at Woolworths £1.49 each. A pound cheaper than John Lewis although made in Korea.

Back at the shop I talked to Mr Becker about training Stephen Blakely to do last fitting. We cleared a space for him. Mr Carpenter cleaned up and while using the vacuum cleaner caught the lead in the revolving wheels of the finishing machine. Luckily no one was hurt. From the loft we brought down a marble table top and a treadle base to be taken home.

In the evening I distributed newsletters and called in on Phil and Mike Gallagher. They had been to California on holiday.

Saturday 12 9 81

We had a lie in until 8.30. A sunny start to the day. After breakfast I tidied up the cuttings Hentschy had left in the rose garden. We had delicious lamb for lunch, and I had a snooze afterwards. I changed the wheel on the car and put the roof rack on. We all drove into London and delivered the German wine and the 1981 Medical directories. Loaded the sewing machine base and the marble table top. The children had a bath and supper on our return. I put out the pewter and silver and made two gallons of beer while listening to Saturday night theatre.

Sunday 13 9 81

Mrs Jardin called in just as we sat down for breakfast. Her husband was shy at first and stayed in the car. The children soon had him out and showed him the garden.

I wanted to pick apples but they were too damp so instead I pruned the prunus.

After lunch we went to pick elderberries on Batchworth Lane. Picked 4 buckets in 40 minutes.

In the evening we made 15 bottles of juice.

Monday 14 9 81

I was keen to get into town punctually because Stephen Blakley was to start last fitting training with Mr Becker. He was already in when I arrived so I settled him in with a mini tour and explained how the Training Manuals were to be used. He seems an understanding type and all went well with him.

It was a quiet morning, just one order for shoes from Mrs Chatfield. She ordered them privately, having been very disappointed with Royal National Orthopaedic Hospital's efforts. We had last made shoes for her in 1975 and had the last and records. Gerald Joyce, book keeper, had the day off. It was unfortunate that it pour down in the afternoon.

I rang Mr Lobb about the shoes for Prince Charles. He said they would cost in the region of £400. I made no comment except I was glad it would be split between the six members of the association. I rang John Wildsmith who was unhappy about the price and said he would pay at cost price. John Carnea was of a similar opinion. I still have to ring the other members and then negotiate with Mr Lobb.

In the evening we called Justine Wodley to help baby sitting and went up to Frithwood school to enroll for badminton. There were only 11 there so Hentschy and I had four games and got the hang of it. We were not out of place without whites. Just plimsolls and a white shirt and slacks.

Tuesday 15 9 81

Travelled up to London on the 8.16 fast Aldgate with Frances Bigger a WI buddy of Mum's and a former Northwood Council of Churches Rep. She has a job envigilating at exams.

It was quiet again at the shop so I could file most of the ladies foot drawings. In the post we had a cheque for a new pair of brown shoes for Graham Lappin.

After lunch I cycled over eleven miles. First to Jermyn Street to see John Carnea. I also saw the Mayor of Westminster as part of the Jermyn St. celebrations. He toured the shops.

St Thomas's Hospital was very quiet and I delivered the shoes for Mrs Earl. Then on to Josh Telfer who was at home even though he did not answer his door. It just pushed open and there he was with his black beard and Rastus hat on. He said he would repay the money I'd lent him to buy settees in larger amounts. It was a waste of time for me really but I gave him Robert Allen's address and maybe he will get some work there.

I went on to Necklinger Mill, Abbey Street and found studio 2. the work shop is large and bright and David Lobb opened the door for me. Robert Allen was at his work bench as was the tall curly headed young man i'd seen before. They made me coffee and were very pleasant and interested in NHS and WEMBA. They may even take some of our surplus sewing machinery. It was about six miles back to the shop and I covered it in twenty five minutes. I had half an hour to go through pattern cutting with Stephen Blakely before home time.

It was a bit of a rush with super to pick up Peter May at 7.15 to go to the Woods committee at Manor Farm Ruislip. Colin Roome from the council was there as was Andrew Wilkinson, David Hawkesworth, chair, Colin Boult, sec. Mr Comey and Mrs Glover. We got through the agenda quickly because there were no disagreements and we have all got to know one another. The main work of getting the plan published is now before us and a series of six meetings before christmas is proposed to cover chapter and verse.

Wednesday 16 9 81

I met Betty Sewell who had the minutes of the Northwood Council of Churches. The post had arrived when I got to the shop. The most interesting letter was from a Muriel Holland who wanted background information about Hollands, the firm my father took over in 1966.

Maggie had done a very good window display. A new red/brown floor cover. A basket of autumn leaves and lambs wool dusters between the shoes. We sold a few dusters through the day. It was quiet at first, but in the late morning the shop was suddenly crowded. One brand new customer. A lady whose shoes had been made by Prior and Howard. She needed them for December. Should be no problem. Mrs Dean came in in tears about shoes from the Royal National Orthopaedic Hospital. She ordered a pair privately from us.

In the afternoon I went over to LFH and Mddx. hospitals and then to Swinard Travel. I had missed the super apex fare by one day and will have to pay more to go to the Orthopaedic shoe conference in Berlin.

Stephen Blakely seems to be settling well and cleared three sections of the shoemaking manual.

Thursday 17 9 81

I had a letter from a 23 year old girl with size 12 shoes asking if we could make for her. I was able to book the orders from yesterday and several people came in for fittings.

in the afternoon I dictated a couple of letters for Shirley to type. Fred Lintott MD of Maxwells rang and confirmed that Lobbs would charge cost price for the shoes for Prince Charles.

An old man came in to have a quote to make one boot. As he was very long winded I upped the price £10 to £130 + VAT. Then I went to Swinards to pay for my ticket. I went on to Lawries in Seymour St. and collected 27 pairs of Vobram sole units. They fitted in to my rucksack and a box on the carrier.

Michael Gleeson sent a letter to Harry Carpenter with a business card. He had LBIST on it, which are what I had after my name. Licensiate of the British Institute of Surgical Technologists. He being now in Ireland had Lepricorn By Instruction to the Shoe Trade. He sounded very happy with life. Fishing and collecting mushrooms in Ireland.

In the evening neighbours Ken Gosden and his wife came round to talk about their Bible Students. The last one did not wash and so smelt the place out. They asked him to leave. The next one seems to be taking them over, so we advised them if they had doubts to call it off before they got too involved.

Friday 18 9 81

A bit more post today, with several cheques and doctors certificates to zero rate VAT. Mrs Skeats from Oxford came to collect her second NHS pair and ordered and paid for a cream coloured pair. Carol Scribbins who had heard about us through the Quaker magazine The Friend came in with photos of handbags that she makes. I tried to work out prices but I was hazy. Maggie our sales assistant goes on holiday next week so I may not be able to sort out how we price handbags to customers. There were several heavy downpours and sun intervals.

I cycled over to the London Foot and Mddx Hospitals and on the way back left a business card at the London Private Hospital in Langham Street.

While Maggie was displaying the hunters bags from Quammer we saw a pearly King and Queen being photographed outside Blagdens the fishmongers on the other side of the road. I took some photos and then invited them in.

The professional photographer was very pleased to use the wall of lasts in the workshop as a background.

Just after they had gone Martin Rose with very flat feet, came in and ordered and paid for a pair to be made with black lizard uppers.

During the morning we had a call from the BBC asking for shoes for a television play with Mary Wimbush. They had found us in Yellow Pages.

Saturday 19 9 81

We had a liesurely breakfast in the dining room, with the best china and silver. Cearals, Frankfurters, current buns and coffee. Afterwards I took the children on the train to Northwood Hills, where at a closing down sale I bought a pair of jeans for £8. Smart but tight. then we bought coffee for Hentschy and stamps for me to use to enrol for the London cycling Campaign. When we got home I made a big fire in the garden with all the branches I'd cut last week from the prunus. I managed to clear the huge heap by lunch time.

Hentschy had cooked beef and cauliflower. Afterwards we went elderberry picking at our usual spot in Batchworth Lane and filled 5 buckets. we made it into juice straight away. I bathed the children and they had super. As a treat they slept on posters in the playroom. We made 21 bottles of juice and were finished by 8.30. We listened to the radio and heard Saturday night theatre. The usual police investigation into a family murder. I bottled my beer into screw top pint bottles I had bought. I hope they don't pop. Put them under the dresser.

Sunday 20 9 81.

During breakfast Michaels second tooth came out. It bled quite a bit but he was too proud to cry. It had been loose since July and we could see the new tooth. The lawn also had many weeks growth on it and took most of the morning to cut. Michael and Jenny were busy picking up cuttings that escaped from the grass box. We also got the leaf sweeper out and cleared a lot more grass with that.

Another session of elderberry picking after lunch. I had to do some climbing and made a spectacular exit from one tree and covered my shirt with red juice. We filled five buckets but did not deal with them in the evening. Instead I went to a United Service at St. Edmund the King. The church was packed. the preacher was very good. Rev. Lewis Mistlebrook. Jesus is Lord was his theme. He had a story about a bible student who got others to tell each other what to preach. After the service there was a wine and cheese party. The posters showing the work of the Council of Churches were displayed. I felt a bit hurt that after asking me to make an announcement Richard Bewes jumped up and made it. Get in quick, that should have been my job as chairman. It was over by 8.30.

Hentschy had cut and washed her hair when I returned and was watching tele.

Monday 21 9 1981

A bright sunny day. Maggie was on holiday so I was at it all the time. answering phones, and seeing customers. Gerald was around a lot of the time and helped. We had an Arab in with a prescription from Mr Power. It said he needed a left raise when in fact he needed a right. I rang up and asked if it was a slip of the pen.

Shirley Joyce travelled back from Baker St with Gerald and me.

The evening was pleasant walking up to the school to play badminton. Only 6 of us so we had plenty of games. The shuttle cock got caught twice in the equipment on the ceiling and I had to climb up the ropes to retrieve it.

Tuesday 22 9 81

It was quiet at first and I could do quite a bit of advising that work was ready. After tea it got busy and we had a continuous stream of people the rest of the day. We had 4 orders including one from Ted Lazarus who haggled as usual, but I think we should make a profit on his new boots. On the train home Stephen Blakey had more good ideas on how to drum up trade. He has a good head for business.

in the evening we had a good session and made 20 bottles of elderberry juice. It is very good for the children.

Wednesday 23 9 1981

Travelled up with Ray. I worked out with Stephen Blakey a way to approach hall porters at hotels. We made a list and rang them for appointments. It was busy all day again in the shop. Mr Brilles came up from Poole but could not wait five minutes for me to finish dealing with a previous client. He had written three letters to say he was coming and then wasted his journey because of his impatience. I slipped out to the Middlesex Hospital with four pairs of shoes and returned just in time to say goodbye to Mrs Jardine who had come in to file my letters and help tidy up.

Mary Wimbush came in with a lady from the BBC. They needed a pair of surgical shoes for a television play. called "By George". I had found an old pair with hole in the soles and quite a high cork. They fitted very well and were happy to take them for £50. Another lady from the BBC had bought in some motorcycle boots which needed letting out with gussets. A massive job and she baulked at £30.

Another new customer ordered shoes. She had heard one of our shoes squeaking at a meeting and the owner complained that hand made shoes should be quiet. Our new customer rushed over and found out where the shoes were made, so our shoes speak for us.

In the evening I went alone to the AGM of the Frithwood School Association. A packed meeting in the community room. The agenda was dealt with quickly and I mentioned the tree planting in the new park.

Thursday 24 9 81

Cloudy weather and later it rained. It matched my mood. We did not take a single order for shoes. Refunded £70 to an Arab lady for a pair of Solidus shoes we raised and the Doctor said was wrong. Stephen Hedley was most moody and no fun to work with. Stephen Blakely spent the afternoon visiting hotels in Park Lane. I hope he was more successful. The newspapers are full of a big fall in share prices. I hope it does not make my trip to Berlin too expensive with a fall in the value of the pound.

Friday 25 9 81

A much better day than yesterday. Betty Sewell's tickets for her holiday had arrived so she was happy. The shop was quiet first thing so I could tidy up and do some advising. We had several heavy showers and so we sold 5 pairs of galoshes, also we sold the last of the leather bags. There were three orders for shoes. One from Mrs Moulding, NHS. One from Mr Gran who is who is always hard to bargain with, but I seemed to mellow him and he agreed the price. Then Mr Makower came in and ordered a straight repeat and paid in advance.

There were plenty of repairs ad foot supports. Mr Bookatz collected his blue and white golf shoes and was delighted.

Hentschy rang at lunch time and reminded me to ring Miss Reynolds to cancel our appointment with her. It was 3.45 before I tried and there was no answer.

I called in at the London clinic to see a teenage girl who needed a raise to her left shoe. I took 3 away, all with horrible PVC soles. I hope our super glue 50/50 will hold.

Saturday 26 9 1981

Plenty of rain. We drove over to Iver to buy plums advertised at a farm. We found that they had not ripened. Instead we bought 56 ponds of potatoes.

Michael and Jenny were invited to a party at Melanies and we drove there because we were late. it brightened up later and Hentschy and I walked into Northwood to look for curtain material. We found some we liked in the little shop on the bridge and ordered it for the front room.

Sunday 27 9 1981

It was sunny. I had a go in the garden picking beans, kohlrabi, and black berries. Cleared the straw out of the strawberries and rolled up the net from the frame roof.

John Orme came and delivered cards for Martin. He told me about Concern.

Mrs Motesiczky came over in the afternoon and took some pictures with the polaroid. She stayed for super. I hope she will paint our portraits. I will pay her with two or three pairs of shoes.

In the evening we cleared up in the rose garden and then in the sitting room we rearranged our records.

Monday 28 9 81

Maggie was back and Gerald was away on holiday. I forgot to take my keys but it didn't matter too much. I used Mr Wilson's to lock up.

We had a busy day with 8 orders, all private. One from Mr Wainwright who last had a pair in 1975.

I went over to the Saudi Health Office for a cheque. The name James Taylor rang bells and I got it in 30 minutes. I was transferred from office to office reasonably quickly.

I am expecting Martin and family to be at home and maybe three bible students.

They were and the children had a great time together.

Tuesday 29 9 81

There were eleven around the breakfast table. The three bible students are very pleasant, Karen from Port Marion, Liz from Pitlochry, and Louise from Watford.

Martin came into town with me. He had several ideas, such as redoing the notice board and fitting an outline of a boot on top.

The layout of the circular also left a lot to be desired and we will do another draft and see if it has more appeal. On the letter heading we can put the directors and their designations at the base.

Mr Joyce showed Martin the books and his impression was that the firm was not doing too badly. We went out for lunch at the Baker and Oven. We had a good serving of chicken and ham pie and half a pint of Worthington for me and a Pepsi for Martin.

Jim Hart, Martins successor in Bangladesh arrived when we got back to the shop and we showed him round. Jim had bought a pair of walking boots at Lawries and we offered to repair them as and when.

After they had left I went on my round to Kuwait Health Office, London Foot and Middlesex Hospital. there I went to the John Astor Ward to measure Michael Turner for a leg iron.

In the evening we had super with the students. Martin and family had left.

Later John Herrning came round to discuss the plans for 12 Eastbury Road. There are various proposals to build extensions and make it into a cramped old peoples home. John and I went round to the Naidoos home and asked if they would host a coffee evening so that we can inform our neighbours. they could then send in a good lot of letters to the planners.

John then invited me to see his house at No 14. They had moved in in a hurry. It felt warm when we entered. He had a computerised heating system, wall insulation and double glazing, bought direct from Alcan. The windows were finished in white.

Hentschy was not happy when I came back. She should have come with me.

Wednesday 30 9 81

It was wet most of the day, but we still took five orders. The most interesting was from a Saudi who ordered zip boots. He ad two body guards and paid in advance.

The morning was fairly quiet with Mrs Tooley coming in with new shoes that were too big.

After lunch I took Mr Rebucks big smelly boot repairs over to Middlesex Hospital and then n to Argyle street to deliver Mr Pedlars repairs. I walked on down Carnaby Street, looked at Oxfam's shop, went into Boots to find a cassette and on to Hamley's new shop. I would love to take the children or Hentschy just for shopping.

When I returned to the shop Mr Meard was in the shop to pay for his new shoes. He is always trying to screw a lower price or quicker delivery. I haven't got the better of him. Today he paid £10 short, but it is not worth fighting for because I pushed his price up well before.

Thursday 1ˢᵗ October 1981.

Another quiet start in the morning with the busy time coming after 11. Mr Becker measured three new lady customers in a row. The first one he nearly lost for us. She was a bit vague and has severe Pes Caves. After lunch I popped down the High Street and bought two metal minature boots at the Oxfam shop for £10 each. Maggie had spotted them. I called at Dentons to see if they would buy my coffee tables. They couldn't as they specialise in glass etc. Looked at the new fish mongers being fitted up where Mac Fish used to be.

I cycled to Prince albert road north of Regents Park to deliver a pair of shoes at the Iraqi Medical Center, then on to see Barry Sullivan at Mornington Crescent. Barry as a child had come to stay weekends and holidays at our home from an orphanage in East Croydon.

When I returned Mr Al Sagar was waiting, hopping up and down. He had been well looked after by Maggie. He ordered two pairs of foot supports, 1 pair of shoes and a stock pair made in error on his lasts.

I rang Eric Lobb and he agreed to charge cost price for Prince Charles's shoes.

In the evening we watched tele. Fanny by Gaslight is developing into a good series.

Friday 2nd October 1981.

It was a bitty morning doing plenty of small jobs that led on. Bob Kochan the maker from Winslow, was in to deliver and collect his work. We had a new customer called Mrs Able who used Able lables on her foot drawings. She had been recommended by a shoe repairer in Finchley Road.

After lunch Mr Mazzola came in. He found his shoes tight. Mr Becker checked his measurements And Mr Mazzola also left shoes for repair. I offer to deliver them to Claridges And he sent the hotel would pay. Most of fire repair them and I rang before I left to confirm. Sure enough cashier Hey me £20 cash Against the invoice. If we can get more work against an easy payment by hotels Also a good. I went on to the Middlesex hospital To deliver invoices and collect orders. I called in at the sewing machine shop called Farros White to see if they could buy our surplus machines. Before we left tonight the man had was round. He looked at them and said he would ring with an offer.

Saturday 3rd October1981

Jenny was not well in the night and slept in our room. She had a tummy upset. After breakfast the Bible students helped me in the garden with pruning. I went into Northwood With my old pushchair to deliver Newspapers and collect our curtain material. I have left my Barclaycard in the shop the week before and had not realised it was missing.

Richardson Dora came over for lunch with Lucy and Kate. The children played well together although Jenny was off-colour. We had a good walk after lunch into Northwood and then round the block.

Sunday 4th October1981

I went to meeting with Michael and has Jenny was still unwell. The ministry was good on the theme of thanks and vision.

In the afternoon I cut the grass, the hedge and the edges with Michael's help. We saw John Harney who gave Michael some wooden figures for kicking balls at and also

Ken Mossop the new owner of Carisbrooke who will come to the neighbours coffee evening.

Monday 5th October 1981

Michael had a bad night. He started at 9 o'clock to be sick and seem to throw up every half hour until 3 o'clock. It was his turn in our room.

The shop was quiet in the morning at around lunch it became busier. In the place we had one order and another confirmed for Mrs Moody. I had a visit from Tony Wills, Managing director of Hawkins. I showed him around the shop with his colleague. Hugh Rossi MP and Minister for the Disabled accepted my invitation to see the shop.

In the evening and Hentschy and I went up to the school to play badminton. There were only four of us so we had a pretty energetic two hours. We invited David from Rofant Road in for a swift beer. We slept like logs and I felt dead all next day.

Tuesday 6th October 1981

The shop was fairly quiet. Only two orders Mrs Sainsbury was very pleased with her boots as was Mrs Rosenberg.In the afternoon I collected the tickets for Hentschy's trip to Hamburg. Went on to collect 8 pairs shoes for Sheik A Leg To be raised and lowered by Friday. Another Arab gave a lot of bother with some raises for a little girl in the London clinic. They love to bargain but by just standing firm they have to give in or loose face.

Woods advisory meeting in the evening. I hope it doesn't take too long.

I felt to ill to go. Headache, and sore throat so I rang Peter May and cried off.

Wednesday 7th October 1981

I felt better after a long sleep And decided I was fit for the visit to Epping Forest with the Royal Forestry Society. Paul Akers rang to confirm he would have a lift with me. I took the children up to school and met Paul and his wife there. I showed him the garden. We reached Epping on the dot. The head conservator and other worthies addressed 60 or so of us in the shelter of the Elizabethan hunting lodge. The weather was clear and glowing. The Lodge had a very clear and impressive museum. We were shown some hornbeam pollards which had been done 20 years ago. They were full cycle, But lack of funds prevented more work. Quite a number of the London group weather and also Andrew Wilkinson MP And a contractor called Tony Collins. Later on He came in my car with Lord Derby. I had met his Lordship on a couple of previous meetings. Five of us in the VW beetle was a good test for it And it's struggled up some of the hills. We were shown several types of Woods. The problem of how to thin recurred frequently. To favour wolves, regeneration or a clean commercial crop? The last site was was one of successful regeneration of beech under Birch, after pollarded beech I've been thinned.

When I got home Hentschy was feeling bad. She went early to bed and I followed at eight.

Thursday 8th October 1981

I could take the children to school again, because we have an appointment at the child guidance centre. We more or less signed off for four months, as Michael is much happier uncontrollable now that we play more with him.

I reached The shop at 10:30. Having bought my annual season to Baker Street. £383 A reduction of £70 off my previous annual. My rates have gone up £89 for six months so I'm still worse off.

It was a bitchy day. For orders yesterday and three today. Mr Carpenter was back from Tenerife looking world hands. Maggie receptionist was on top form droning on and on. I will have to put the plug in it. Gerald had worked out the months balances for private Customers.Five stick And I rang the industrial society to ask what to do. To work cases who had paid money on account and have not come and 430, And Others were in dispute, but not straightforwardly. It was a case of consumerism in reverse.

I've brought a pair of last time to hang in the garden shed for Mrs E Scarlett, and hold Sikora. I had delivered her shoes earlier onto the Middlesex hospital.

At eight I went round to number 10 E. rewrote our other Half of the house.We had the new residents of Number 14 and Carisbrooke. Judy Deakin and Mrs Naylor Smith were also there. We agreed to all write letters to modify the planning application for number 12 so that we could see an old peoples Home of the sort it used to be. An upmarket home for the elderly and not a knackers yard, crammed with old bodies

Friday, 9 October 1981

And morning full of bits with no orders. A man from Pieroth wines called in to give a tasting. I had decided on what I wanted beforehand and did not let myself be tempted into more. He was a good talker And Maggie and Mr Wilson had a sip. Jack Hirsch rang and told me about the efforts of the Royal National Orthopaedic Hospital to make shoes for him. Success after eight months, but he still wants to come back. I have an appointment to see and Mrs Harding on Monday, having had a recommendation from her Dr Rogers. I wrote a letter to the planning department about number 12 Eastbury Road and I hope Hentschy will write one as well.

Stephen Blakely and I went by bus to see Mr Daheen at the Hilton Hotel on Park Lane. He bought two pairs of Dru shoes and ordered a pair of made-to-measure. He paid cash from the case full of money. A lovely sight. When I got back Joy Palmer ordered a pair of long boots and agreed to pay £50 more for high uppers.

Saturday 10th October 1981

We take 60 pounds of apples and put them on trays on the loft. In the afternoon Michael and I worked in the garage taking nails out of battons and Cuprinoling them. In the evening Hentschy and I cleared out our wardrobe and dismantled it.. We stored it in the front bedroom. It was a fairly big job.

Sunday, 11 October 1981

A bright day and one for the garden again. The wind had broken about from the Chestnut tree and it had fallen on the telephone wire to Carisbrooke. Ken Fossett our new neighbour came aKeep putting Wnd helped me to rescue his wires. After lunch the Bible students helped spreading leaf mould and I dug over several parts to clear weeds. We also cut back quite a few bushes in the rose garden. In the evening I put up the Secondary glazing with Hentschy over the five windows that we liked to open.

Monday 12th October 1981

Met Betty Sewell on the train after her trip to Agadir. She had not been thrilled by it. It was a bitting day and cold. Just to orders, one from a lady in Scotland who was recommended by McAfee Maybe trouble with narrow feet and mind. In the afternoon I went round yet again to Mr Maguire's office in Robert Adams Street. He was still not comfortable and nitpicking. My patience will last longer than his. I went on to deliver my letters to Shirley at the British Council. A big block in Portland Place.

In the evening I went on to chair a meeting of the Northwood Council of churches. Hentschy gave Ron Turner, Mrs Hyman and me a lift to Joel Street. Hentschy went on to play badminton. How are adverts at the Bible college for 6 more people So that helped to keep the badminton class going.

The council meeting had a lot of ideas and flowed well. We found a way to help young unemployed through the efforts the Methodist Church and it could be one of the more positive things that the council has inspired.

Monday 13th October 1981

Another bitchy day. Arabs come in and trying on shoes and then not wanting to pay for them. I had a call from the Ministers of the Disabled secretary to say she would let our local MP know of the proposed visit. I wonder if I should let the media know? We could make some wind out of it. Had another call for stage shoes but nothing has come of it.

In the evening Hentschy and I went to the school. As usual Michaels teacher had plenty to say about his lack of concentration And we will try to help him with his writing. Jenny was very good according to a teacher and doing well.

Back home I started on fitting the batton on the ceiling on our bedroom. I did the sides and the middle. The big screwdriver helped a lot.

Tuesday 14th October 1981

It was pretty quiet most of the day. Mr Johanna from Kuwait came and ordered two pairs and haggled as usual. Mrs Glynis Dean also came in with a letter from Mr Borges of the Royal National Orthopaedic Hospital in which she accused our firm of Bad practices. It could be liable. I wrote asking for an explanation or I could take it up with the Minister when he calls. I delivered a pair of shoes for Mr smells of Middlesex hospital Which is looking a lot cleaner with its scrubbed walls. 49 Tottenham Street is for sale has ever and I wonder who will take it. I cycled onto Anderson's timber merchant at Islington Green and ordered the wood for our bedroom. I paid £211 pounds cash and it will be delivered next Wednesday. On my return I looked at Camden passage and its antique shops.

Back at the shop I rang Ian Sherwood of the trade association and told him about the ministerial visit and the letter from the Royal National Orthopaedic Hospital. Mr Lobb rang me to say that shoes for Prince Charles were ready. I agreed a date with the West End Master Boot maker's Association Members. I will have to get a list of members typed up. We will view the shoes at Lobbs premises on October 26.

Wednesday 15th October 1981

A busy day because I'm going to Berlin in the evening on an international orthopaedic shoe makers conference. I packed everything in a large black holdall so I wouldn't have any suitcases to wait for. In the morning I went first to the shop and sorted out a few things out. At 9:45I left with Stephen Blakely and took a taxi to Camden Town To a seminar of the Foot Health Council. Dr David Owen arrived just before us and was the opening speaker. He pointed out the ageing population and the need to keep it mobile. This point was echoed by other speakers, and at one point I spoke to say shoes that were made-to-measure where the ideal.

After lunch Stephen and I circulated giving out cards when we could. Spencer Crocker and then gave a lively and good talk, but the Chairman Lewis Schmidt forgot to thank him. A talk that was read about shoe fitting was boring, but the last one by Tony Mcnab on sports footwear was very good.

I left the King's fund centre at 3:30. Hopping straight into a cab to Baker Street station and caught a Watford train immediately and was home by 4.10. Very good. Had a cup of tea with the family and then we drove to the airport where I flew British Airways to Berlin via Hannover. Met a top-class photographer on the plane who could talk. I Cut decided not to take a taxi at the bus and that took me to the Kaiser Damm where I eventually found my hotel Am Studio. I have a pleasant clean room. Much better than the one in Paris two years ago.

Thursday 16th October1981

Hi did not sleep well because I kept wondering what time it was. Not having an alarm clock bothered me. Breakfast was served on the seventh floor where there was an good view. It was buffet style and the tables were rather tight. A Japanese man sat at my table. As short walk brought me to the conference centre I could book in. An exhibition of prizewinners was in the foyer showing shoes etc. At 9 o'clock A senator gave a welcome talk. It was a very comprehensive exhibition. I could order or actually buy all the things on my shopping list. Lasting pincers, foot in printers, eyelets and buckles and oval grain lizard. Standard engineering was there to demonstrate its lasting machine.

A good lunch and then a series of lectures. First on the theme of drop foot and cosmetic calipers. I made a point about the calibre that needed a high heel, to say that the other shoe would need adjustment. The lecturer said it was obvious and the chairman said it was a small points that make a correct shoe. In the evening we went to the Kranzler cafe for a good meal but it was to full. Although I could get in because I have a ticket I couldn't find anywhere to sit.

There were long queues for the self-service buffet and not much left when I got there, just sauerkraut and sausages for my main course. I squeezed in on the end of a table of people from Aachen and then joined another lot from Heidelberg. Peter Shaw and Jerry Dudley were still with Mr Pfeiffer. The Heidelberg group decided to see some night life so I went with them to a famous night dive called the Ku dork. Three marks to go in with a token to exchange for food and drink. I kept mine and just pushed through room after room of hot smoky noise. It was an experience but not a pleasant one. I left and lost the people I was with and met another lot including a couple from Berlin. We went to look for a quieter bar. Opposite as strip club I saw a glass shop with a man working making drinking glasses. Next door was a pub that look inviting and it connected with the Glass shop. We looked and talked the glassmaker And I mentioned I collected little shoes. The lady from Berlin asked if he could make me one. We had some beers and they had cocktails and then we went back to the worker who have made of glass shoe with laces. I asked him how much I owed him and he said a Paddy, that is an Irish whiskey. The lady persuaded him to make her one as well.

Friday 17th October 1981

Dad died 13 years ago today. I rang Hentschy and she sounded as miserable as expected. Being left at home. It was a solid morning of lectures followed by another lot after lunch on spasticity and various ways to cope. At the very end I managed to ask a couple of questions on delivery time and durability of the shoes on growing children. 3 to 4 weeks and they lost about a year. At the exhibition I met shoemakers from Hamburg and I also went round to the Standard Engineering exhibit. I met the whole of the Jane

Saunders and Manning Team. They are a desperate trio needing work. Highly mechanised and so overcapacity is their problem. I have heard that the Television tower was worth the trip for two marks so I walked round and went up. It was pretty seeing all the lights, a fairground and the huge road layout near by.

This evening is the grand do with Dinner jackets. There were performances from singers, two bands and some children who danced a Mozart quartet and gave out the forest of long stemmed roses to the ladies. I had a few dances and drank a whole bottle of Rhine wine.

Many more years of diary entries. These may become available on Amazon.

Printed in Great Britain
by Amazon

85037850R00129